# PAPA X-RAY

**Jim Lang**

*To Dennis & Dorothy all the best!*

**Published by:**
**Happy Landings**

## Other books by Jim Lang:

*Make Your Own Breaks - Become an Entrepreneur & Create Your Own Future*
Published by DBM Publishers in New York and Trifolium Books in Toronto. To order Make Your Own Breaks and its companion Instructor's Guide: In Canada: In Toronto: 416-213-1919 ext. 1999... Ontario & Quebec: 800-387-0141. Other provinces: 800-387-0172. In the U.S.: 800-805-1083
Fax orders for all areas, Canada & U.S.: 416-445-5967.

*Great Careers for People Who Want to be Entrepreneurs:* Published by Trifolium Books and Weigl Educational Publishers Ltd. This is the first careers book on entrepreneurship written for high school students. To order: 800-668-0766

## Canadian Cataloguing in Publication Data

**PAPA X-RAY**                    Lang, Jim, 1947 -

ISBN 0-9697322-5-2

1. Lang, Jim, 1947-   2. Bush pilots - Northwest Territories - Biography.  3. Teachers - Northwest Territories - Biography. I. Title

TL540.L295A3 1998     629.13'092     C98-901213-1

Editing: Angela Dobler                    Cover Art: Kelly Brine
Layout and Typesetting: Happy Landings
Written and produced in Canada

**Published by:**
**Happy Landings**           **Tel.: 613-269-2552**
**RR # 4**                   **Fax: 613-269-3962**
**Merrickville, Ontario**    **Web site: www.happylanding.com**
**Canada, K0G 1N0**          **E-mail: books@happylanding.com**

# Contents

# About Papa X-Ray

*Papa X-Ray* is the lighthearted, true story of a trusty old airplane, a family adjusting to life in the far north and a greenhorn pilot learning to fly in the spectacular ruggedness of Canada's Northwest Territories.

In 1985, Jim Lang, his wife Mary and young son Johnny moved to Nahanni Butte, Northwest Territories. He took a job teaching in a one-room school. The only year-round access to the isolated community was by airplane so he bought one. Then he learned to fly. Over the next three years, Lang led the family on airborne adventures that would last a lifetime.

Ride along with the family as they fly their 1966 four-seat, single-engine Cessna everywhere from weekly grocery runs to trips across Canada.

"Lang is masterful at placing his readers in that fourth seat and making them laugh."

*Garth Wallace*
*aviation humorist*

# *Foreword*

For as long as I can remember, I have worshipped airplanes. I have always regretted being born too late to witness the squadrons of Harvards and Bolingbrokes that filled the prairie skies during the war. In those glory days Saskatchewan was dotted with airfields. Hundreds of planes and pilots practised bombing over Quill Lake, just to the north of our farm, returning to Dafoe to refuel and reload.

By 1955 only a few occasional bombers passed high overhead, droning off to places infinitely more exciting than our postage stamp farm, far below. Bare feet planted in the warm summer fallow, I shielded my eyes, scanning for the source of that sound. There! A silver speck twenty thousand feet up glinted in the blazing sky. I fell back in the dirt and lay there, my imagination following its droning progress to somewhere I'd rather be — anywhere. I was eight years old.

Some day, I vowed, I am going to fly.

*Jim Lang*

# Acknowledgements

I wrote Papa X-Ray about ten years ago, mostly to amuse my wife, Mary, who read each chapter as it appeared. She laughed at the funny bits, corrected lapses of memory and factual errors and encouraged me to keep on writing. Thank you, Mary. A publisher rejected the manuscript so I let it gather dust for several years until our good friend Betsy Odegaard phoned one day. She'd been re-reading the yellowing pages and she encouraged me to return to the project. Thank you, Betsy. I reworked the stodgy prose a little and decided to send it off to Doris Ohlmann at the Canadian Owners and Pilots Association publication, *Canadian Flight*, and she promptly began to print monthly installments. Thank you, Doris. COPA members wrote letters to me and to the editor saying they liked the stories. Thank you, COPA readers. Garth Wallace took note of the interest and suggested turning the stories into the book you hold in your hands. Thank you, Garth.

Finally, I want to thank the people who appear in this book, all of whom are real — though one or two have been given new names. I hope they'll accept my recollection of events as close enough to the truth. At least, close enough for a pilot.

*Jim Lang*
*September, 1998*

# Chapter One

# Air taxi

"Just pull the truck up to the hangar. We'll unload it on the floor there first and then into the plane," a young ramp man shouted to my open window.

I drove up to the Simpson Air building next to the gravel air strip and we created a neat pile of suitcases and boxes on the hangar floor.

"Now, what about the freezer?" I mused.

*"The freezer?"* He was startled.

"No, no, I don't mean the *whole freezer*," I laughed, "just the three or four hundred pounds of meat, milk and other stuff in it. Frozen."

He jumped into the big GMC's box, opened the freezer door, looked in, dropped the lid, jumped out and pointed at the aircraft.

"Two loads," he pronounced. "No way we'll get you there in one load." Seeing my look, he added, "Don't worry, the Department of Education will pay for the move. It's part of your contract. Now who and what goes first?"

I thought for a few seconds. "Mary and Johnny go first with the frozen goods. The food would just thaw out here while we waited for your return trip. Let's get the goods into the freezer at Nahanni Butte as quick as we can...okay?"

Mr. Simpson Air nodded. "Okay. And, by the way, it's pronounced 'Nahanni', to rhyme with granny. You don't want to sound like a southerner, eh?"

A southerner! I pictured dozens of campsites from Red Deer to Regina, Dallas to Los Angeles, Guelph to Edmonton – mental postcards from our years in the music business. And now, August, 1985, the period at the end of our nomadic sentence: Fort Simpson. Who's he calling a yokel?

After more than two years on the road, our son Johnny was a veteran traveler. He was weaned, potty-trained and spoke his first word, "Babu!" in our 32-foot Glendale travel trailer. I was glad he was too young to feel any sense of loss when we'd unloaded the amplifiers, speakers, cases, light stands and boxes, all stenciled, "Lang & Ackroyd Band." Our sound equipment would not be coming with us on this gig. This time my audience would be a gaggle of elementary school students in a place called Nahanni Butte in Canada's Northwest Territories and Mary's would be an audience of one.

"Oh, boy, Johnny! An airplane ride! I can hardly wait!" Mary bubbled as she bundled Johnny into the Britten-Norman Islander and took her place in the right seat while the ramp man continued loading our boxes. Trim, athletic and ready for any new adventure, Mary fairly beamed with excitement. A proper husband would likely have taken this moment to be grateful for being blessed with such a fine mate. And I would have too, had I not been transfixed by the prospect of getting a ride in this lovely airplane. I felt a strong pang of envy.

"You Jim Lang?" a woman shouted from the office. "You got a telephone call!"

I ran into the Simpson Air waiting room and took the phone. It was Margaret from the Department of Education office up the hill from the strip.

"Jim, I just talked to the store in Nahanni and they're hoping you could fly in some pop they ordered."

"No problem, Margaret, let 'em know I'm bringing it in!"

Pop for the kids! That would get me off on the right foot. I visualized their grateful faces, no doubt starved for the exotic soft drinks that I will have ferried in more than a hundred miles by air – just to make them happy. I scooted back to the plane and helped the ramp man finish piling in the last of the cross-rib roasts.

"Say, do you have some pop that's supposed to go to Nahanni?" I asked, glancing into the hangar, innocently.

"Yeah, there's some here, I think."

"Let's throw it on, whaddaya say? I said we'd bring it in."

He stopped and eyed me coldly. Oops, I thought, I think I've crossed some kind of line here. But, what could the problem be? This was a big plane with a little room left and, well, a few cans of pop shouldn't be a problem.

I followed him as he walked over to the hangar and pointed to twelve flats of no-name cola and orange soda.

"I see," I said.

He turned to me and in that moment I realized that he was not only the ramp man, he was also the pilot. This was the north, after all, where pilots still got their hands dirty.

"I don't want to be rude, but let's be clear here," he said coolly. "I say what goes on the plane and what doesn't. Pop is heavy. It goes with your trip, not this one." He smiled a forced smile and strode off toward the plane.

Yikes, that hurt! Just like some over-zealous fan in the music business days. I yearned to be an "airplane groupie" and now that I was about to get a ride in a plane, the pilot had to put me in my place. Ah, well. I sat down on the GMC's tailgate to watch the Islander line up for takeoff. I could see Mary's smiling face through the windshield and Johnny strapped in behind her, his head rotating like a periscope. The offended pilot applied full power and with prop-blasted gravel spraying behind the two engines, the high-wing twin roared down the strip, climbed out, arced to the west and flew out of sight.

I looked at my watch. Hmmm. Two hours to kill. I might as well head back to the Department of Education office and get some more orientation. It had been ten years since I'd set foot in a classroom. I couldn't very well get up in front of my students next Monday and announce, "And now here's a little tune we stole from Charlie Daniels...hit it, Mary!"

It was a short stroll back up to the ugly, two-storey, corrugated steel government building. Function obviously spoke louder than form up here – at least when it came to industrial construction. I took in the community as I sauntered up the hill. There were small, pleasant houses, Honda trikes, dogs barking and occasional evidence of the thirteen hundred souls who inhabited Fort Simpson. Of these the Dene formed the largest group. The Dene had called this land home for more than ten thousand years...*ten thousand years*.

To the east, I could see the sun glinting on the mighty Mackenzie River, fat with silty water from the Liard and Nahanni Rivers, flowing north to Inuvik and the Arctic Ocean, thousands of miles away. As broad as a lake, it was a huge river, which was likely why the Dene called it Deh Cho – "Big River." It was the ribbon that bound dozens of bands throughout this part of the Northwest Territories. Altogether they numbered fewer than 15,000 people. Their villages and towns dotted a mass of land larger than most countries on Earth, this great northern land –

9

Denendeh. I took a deep breath of the cool clean air. I had a very good feeling about our decision to move here.

I was dreaming. "Somebody get that phone!" An invisible telephone rang and rang. "Why doesn't somebody get that phone?"

There. It stopped. Thank heavens, I thought. A sharp pain wracked my ribs. Now I was being attacked. "What's going on?"

"Jim, wake up! *Wake UP!*"

I sat bolt upright. Mary was shaking me and shoving the receiver into my hand at the same time.

"What the... For crying out loud! Who'd call a musician at this hour?" I stared at the bedside clock. "It's only ten-thirty in the morning!" The room came into focus. "Where are we?"

"Athabasca," Mary said.

"Uh, Athabasca? Oh yeah, Athabasca Inn. Okay. I'm awake."

"It's Margaret, the education consultant and Steve, the superintendent in Fort Simpson. Remember?" Mary hissed urgently. "They're going to interview you for the job."

Right! Of course! I had arranged the call. "Well, here goes nothing, sweety!"

I took the telephone, settled back on the pillow and searched desperately for my, "I'm awake, really, I'm awake!" voice.

"Hello?"

Mary settled in next to me, twisting the receiver so she could hear both sides of the conversation that would change our lives forever.

"Hello, Jim, I'm Steve and I'm here with Margaret."

"Hi, Jim!"

"Hello, both of you. I'm glad to hear from you." Mary squirmed to listen in, smiling conspiratorially.

"Jim, I just want to make sure you understand what this job entails," Margaret began. "You'd be going into a village of about 75 people to teach in a one-room school, Kindergarten to Grade Eight." She paused. "That doesn't scare you?"

"Not at all," I replied, "both Mary and I attended one-room schools in communities just as small, if not remote, and I taught in one for a year in British Columbia. I like one-room schools."

"About your previous teaching experience, then," Steve continued, "so you have taught before?"

Okay, I thought, we're at square one, here.

"Yes, for a year, um, ten years ago."

"Ten years ago, I see..."

"Yes, well, I realize I haven't taught for some time, but, heck, how much have one-room schools and kids changed?" I laughed, hopefully.

"I'm surprised you want to leave the music business," Margaret said, now testing me. "It sounds like a lot of fun."

"Actually, it is. And it's a lot of work, too. We've enjoyed it but we're finding it's just too much with our young son on the road every week. We're ready for a change."

"I hope you realize just how much of a change you'd be in for up here," Margaret laughed.

Mary poked me and whispered, "What does she mean?"

"Now, for your qualifications," Steve cut in, "I gather you have a degree?"

"Lots of 'em," I chuckled. "And about time I put them to use, too. I haven't found my masters degree in Philosophy of Education overly useful as a country singer!"

"I see," Steve replied, perhaps sounding a bit more shocked than I'd have liked. "So, tell me, Jim, do you think you can handle this job?"

"I'd love to have the opportunity to try, Steve. I'll be fair, there aren't a lot of teaching positions going begging for guys like me who've been out of the classroom for so long. I realize it sounds like I want this job because it's the only one I can get, but the truth is, I tend to want what other people don't want. If I could choose any kind of teaching job, I'd choose a one-room school. I just think they're a great place to learn and to teach. Now, are ya gonna hire me or what?" They both laughed loudly.

"We'll call you in a day or so with our decision," Steve replied. "Now go back to sleep."

I wondered how he knew we were in bed.

I hung up the phone and noticed Mary looking pensive – and quite fetching. I snaked my way over to her side of the bed.

"Did it sound as though they thought we were a little crazy to take this job?" she asked, ignoring me. I slumped.

"Yes, it did," I mumbled. "And that means we're the right people for it."

Margaret phoned the next day to tell me I had the job. I wasn't surprised, but I was a little relieved. Later we told the boys in the band. They were stoic. We still had three months of work to play out and that was longer than most bands lasted start to finish.

I trotted up the steps past the Royal Bank and into the offices of the Government of the Northwest Territories.

"Jim, you're still here!" Margaret exclaimed as I strolled into the education office.

"Yeah, Mary and the kid just took off with the first load. I'll be on the next flight so I have some time to kill…"

"The 'kid'!" Margaret scolded. "You mean Johnny."

"Yeah, all right, Johnny, already. Hey, we come from the music biz. We call a kid a kid, ya know?"

She smiled and shook her finger at me. "Did the pop get loaded for Jayne at the store?"

"No," I answered, blushing a little as I recalled my gaffe. "It's going in with me. I hope they appreciate it when it arrives." I waved off her quizzical look, "I'll tell you about it another time..."

Margaret was the education consultant for the Fort Simpson area and I was part of her caseload. I would soon learn to appreciate her talents, as she would save me from myself many times. We sat down to chat.

"Since I have a little more time, I thought I'd wring your brain a bit more."

"Wring away!" she laughed.

"Okay," I began, settling into a chair by her desk, "how many students, which grades, what resources?"

"From what we can tell, you'll have about 27 students, from Kindergarten to Grade Eight – in one room, for now." She saw my startled look. "I know it sounds like a heavy load, but some of the Grade Sevens and Eights will likely end up here in Fort Simpson at Deh Cho Hall later this fall, and you'll have Laura, the best classroom assistant in these parts."

"Twenty-seven in one room? Yikes! I wish we'd had audiences that big at some of our gigs!"

"Yeah, right," she laughed. "Well, you'll have a full house in this club, all right, but the new school is almost finished. You'll be meeting Duffy when you get in later today. He's the contractor and I think the only non-Slavey in the settlement."

"Not counting Mary, *Johnny* and me, I guess." I stifled my instinct to call him "the kid" and glanced at my watch. "They should be there by now, the lucky stiffs."

"Why are they so lucky?"

"'Cause they got to fly first," I mimicked a whine.

"Oh, so you like airplanes, do you? Well, you'll get your share of flying in up here, my boy."

"You don't like airplanes?" I shot her a look of mock horror.

"Oh, I like airplanes, all right," she sighed. "It's just that we kind of take them for granted around my house. I guess you haven't met my husband, Paul. He's been flying commercially up here for decades and he's a complete airplane nut. Better not let him near you," she laughed.

Then she pointed to a burly, bearded man in the corner office. "That's Ron, the local head of the Department of Public Works. You talked to him on the phone, but you haven't met him." She took me by the arm. "He wanted to see you before you left, so you're in luck," she said, walking me across the room. "You'll want to get to know him because he's the guy who oversees your house fuel, fridge, stove and pretty much everything that the government provides for you in your contract. Go on, he won't bite."

I wasn't so sure. He looked pretty gruff and was barking loudly at someone about a furnace fan motor. Ron waved me in and hung up the phone in one smooth movement.

"Teachers! Don't know a furnace blower from a…well, anyhow, you'd be Jim Lang," he said, extending his hand. His face betrayed a friendly smile. I was ready to retreat into an excuse about being a musician, more than a teacher, but before I could speak he continued. "So, did you get your trailer parked all right? Enough room in the yard?"

"Lots of room, thanks."

He changed gears. "Let me get this straight. You left the music business to move to Nahanni Butte to teach in a one-room school, is that right?"

"Guilty as charged," I nodded. "We had a really good run at the business, had a great time, made decent money and traveled pretty much everywhere there are roads, which left…"

"Nahanni Butte?" He was incredulous. I squirmed a little. He made the place sound like Devil's Island. "Why? I mean, really. I can see somebody leaving Nahanni Butte to go into the music business, but not the other way around!"

"Well, even with that big trailer and our nanny, the road's not the best place to raise a kid. He's probably been in more bars than you have, and he's only two and a half!"

"I wouldn't jump to conclusions," Ron laughed. "You don't know me all that well yet!" His expression turned more serious.

"Do you have any idea…any idea *at all* about where you're going?"

The question caught me off guard. Ron launched into a sermon for southern greenhorns. "First off," he continued, indicating my jeans and sweatshirt, "you're over-dressed."

I laughed. He was beginning to remind me of the gruff, but friendly farmers I grew up with in Saskatchewan.

"No, I'm serious. It's been raining in Nahanni and it's going to be muddy."

He saw my "big deal" expression. His voice took on fatherly overtones. "Jim, I see guys like you every year. You come up from the south and get yourselves into places like Nahanni Butte and within six months you're crawling the walls, trailing drool and wondering why you ever agreed to go there."

He leaned forward and spoke intently. "You don't know it yet, but I'm your friend. I want you to know what you're getting into. When your furnace goes cold and it's midnight and forty-five below, you can't pick up a phone and call for a repairman – or a doctor if your kid gets an earache." He ticked his points off on his fingers. "First, because there are no phones, except the radiophone in the store and second because there's no way to get to you in the middle of the night, because the strip isn't lit at Nahanni – and if the weather is down there's no way to get to you period."

He had my attention now. "If that boy of yours wanders more than forty feet east of your house he'll drop off a sheer cliff into the Nahanni River." He smiled mischievously, "And it's cold, fast and deep."

He paused for effect then switched to the "good cop" mode. "It is a beautiful place, Nahanni Butte is, kind of like a Banff, tucked into the mountains and tall timber but this isn't a Walt Disney movie. Nature has a very cold heart. It can eat you alive out there. I just want to make sure you really know where you're headed."

"I appreciate you being candid with me," I ventured, walking on eggs, "but we're not babes in the woods. I grew up on a farm without electricity. Mary and I have lived in other isolated communities and really enjoyed them. I've spent much of my life in the company of native people, so I'm rather looking forward to the challenge."

"The challenge!" Ron burst out laughing. "It'll be that, Jimmy lad! Don't say I didn't warn you! Remember, you're not getting the isolation bonus for nothing!"

14

"Frankly, I love the fact that we're going to be isolated. It means more airplane rides!"

"Airplanes!" Ron snorted. "I suppose you have some romantic notion about pilots, too! Glorified taxi drivers, that's all they are!" Ron rose to see me out. "You know, Jim, I don't want you to take me the wrong way. I'd actually love to see someone like you stay for awhile. It's just that, well, in my experience it doesn't happen all too often." He pointed to a large box on the floor. "I'm sending in this new furnace gun next week, so you'll have a spare." He looked me in the eye, "I'd be really pleased if you'd learn how to install it yourself. Think you can handle that?"

"We'll see," I shook his hand. "Maybe Mary, the kid and I will surprise you."

"I hope you will. It would certainly be a welcome surprise, I'll say that much."

By the time I trotted back to Simpson Air, the Islander was already parked. The sandy-haired pilot was waiting for me.

"Well, you'll be happy to know I left your wife and son safely at the end of the strip at Nahanni Butte and we'd better get a move on if we're going to make this return trip today." He glanced at the sun. "Ready to load her up?" he asked.

Was that a friendlier tone creeping into his voice? Maybe he'd forgiven me for my earlier faux pas.

"Well, as the guys in the band used to say, 'work gets done faster when somebody's doin' it!'" I started chucking boxes at him and he packed them into the bowels of the Islander.

"You had a band?" he asked, suddenly quite interested.

As we worked, I served him up some of the juicier stories from our years on the road. We were on veritable "buddy" terms by the time we climbed into the cockpit. The flats of pop were the last pieces loaded and they raised not a ripple of comment.

As the only passenger, I took the right seat. Wow! Gauges and dials and knobs all over the place! I took the headset he offered, put it on and immediately started peppering him with questions.

"Tell you what, hotshot," he chuckled, "just let me get this thing in the air and then we'll have plenty of time to talk airplanes!" I wasn't about to risk his good will, so I shut right up and drank in every movement he made, flicking switches, pulling knobs and talking in some foreign language to invisible people out there in aviation-land, somewhere.

15

"Yowza!" I shouted as he applied full power.

He shot me a curious look while he rotated the airplane off the gravel strip.

Hmmm, I thought. Maybe Ron had something there. This guy does look a little like a jaded cab driver. Impossible! Listen to that roar, and look! We're airborne! No taxi I've ever ridden in can do this! There's Fort Simpson disappearing below us and there's...oh my God, hundreds of miles of bush and lakes!

We were traveling in a three-dimensional postcard. Ahead, a solid carpet of green, dotted with silver lakes. To the left, the Liard River was a sinewy line snaking westward ahead of us, paralleling our track.

"See that flat mountain on the right up there?" he pointed dead ahead.

I quickly spotted the unusual shape among the diamond-toothed range of mountains that rose up on the horizon a hundred miles away.

"That's the butte. As you can see, it's not hard to find – in good weather," he added, matter-of-factly.

The magnificence of the view overwhelmed me, diverting my attention from airspeed indicators, ADFs and altimeters. I stared down at the moving picture below. We've really done it this time, I thought. Once we set those wheels in motion, there was no stopping the events unfolding in their wake. My eyes glazed, vivid memories flooded my mind.

"You seem to be enjoying this." The young pilot broke into my half-sleep. My eyes came into focus on the mountains ahead, now much closer. "Beats me why you'd want to move up here."

"Why do you say that?" I countered and noticed he didn't seem to hear me. He looked at me and said, "You gotta keep that mike close to your lips, Bud." I adjusted the microphone on the green headset and repeated my question.

"Because," he went on, "I've been up here for a year now, and from what I've seen, the only people who move up here from the south are losers who can't make it anywhere else."

I was shocked. "And you?"

"I'm only here to build hours, then I'm gone."

Well, I thought, now there's an interesting attitude. I wonder how many pilots shared that cynical point of view?

As the mountains drew closer, I thought it a great pity that he could fly in this paradise and not see the beauty around him. How could he not simply love flying, no matter where he flew?

16

The Liard curved off to the south and joined the Nahanni River, flowing from the north. As we began our descent, I paid more attention to the scene below than to the pilot and plane. It seemed we had little in common, after all. To the north, the butte was right in my face, a sheer wall of rock, flat on top like a marine's crew cut. At its foot, I saw a few reddish buildings.

"That's the Nahanni National Park headquarters," the pilot announced, perhaps feeling a little guilty at unloading on me earlier. "There's a short strip over there, too. Sometimes we fly in there, but it's a tight squeeze."

I caught a glimpse of the strip, blinking in and out among the stands of birch and spruce. Suddenly the river was below us and then...there it was, Nahanni Butte.

We blasted over the scattered buildings, my head craned to take in as much as I could in one pass. I saw a road leading from the village and followed to where it met the north end of the strip. There was an old truck parked there, with somebody leaning against it, looking up at us. We turned south, then east, and lined up for the landing. Wow, the runway was narrow, just a gray line between tall stands of timber. There was not much room for error here, either, with the butte sitting like a giant granite Buddha right off the north end. If we missed the approach – splat!

The wheels touched and we rumbled and rolled to the end. The plane ride was over and I felt a little deflated. I wouldn't mind being one of these "taxi drivers", no sir!

I jumped out right into the face of Grizzly Adams, or so he seemed. Long, tousled hair, beard and big grin, this guy looked like a real northerner.

"I'm Duffy and you're Jim, right?" He extended his hand.

"Glad to meet you. Are you the welcoming committee?" I laughed. He didn't.

"It seems so," he said, with a resigned tone. "I rescued your wife and son earlier."

"Rescued? Are they all right?" I was a little concerned. It was his turn to laugh.

"Yeah, they're fine. I heard this plane come in earlier and waited to see if it was the new teacher. After a half hour, I decided I'd better come out and take a look. I found your wife and – Johnny, is it?" I nodded. "Anyway, I found them sitting on a pile of frozen groceries that was melting fast, so I hauled them and the cargo to your house. I guess nobody else thought to meet them." His voice trailed off. "It would have made a lot more sense..." he

17

added, now talking directly to my jaded young pilot, who was busy dumping my gear on the gravel.

The pilot stopped and listened.

"As I was saying, it would have been a lot easier if you'd taxied into the village, like Simpson Air always does, instead of dumping her here."

"Let's have some help getting this unloaded," the pilot said. "I have to get going."

We packed Duffy's old truck until it looked like the front wheels might take air. The Islander departed and not another word passed between the pilot and me. I never saw him again.

"Too bad you got such a jerk," Duffy commented as we climbed into the ancient Chevy halfton. "Most of the pilots up here are really good guys. But, you'll find that out soon enough."

"Glad to hear it. I thought maybe it was just me."

"Naw. I'm a pilot, too – although I haven't gotten my licence updated for a few years," he offered.

The engine fired up in a cloud of blue smoke and we lurched up the access road to the village. On closer inspection, I could see he wasn't as old as I'd first thought. Maybe mid-thirties. Was that an American accent?

"I love flying," he said. "Hope you do."

"Can't get enough of it."

"You're going to like it here, then. You'll get plenty of flying, for sure."

We passed a row of three huge storage tanks surrounded by a chain link fence and a ditch. "That's the tank farm. You've got about five hundred thousand litres of diesel and gasoline combined. The diesel is for the generating station there." He pointed out the blue metal building as we passed, smoke pouring from its exhaust stack. I could hear the big generator roaring away inside. "It's also for your furnace and the school's."

We pulled into the centre of the settlement. "This is the store on the right, the nursing station on the left, your old school dead ahead and," he turned right, "the new school that I'm building for you is over there." He pointed to a large rectangular log structure rising among the houses. "And this," he poked me to look, "would be your wife and son standing in front of your new house."

There they were, running out to meet me. Behind them a lovely brown log house sat a few yards from the river bank, just as Ron had said.

18

"Jim, you're here," Mary said. "Thanks, Duffy, I don't know what we'd have done without you."

I gave my little family a big hug and was about to check out the house, when I remembered the flats of pop.

"Just a minute. You said that was the store over there?" He nodded. "I'll be right back."

I ran over to the store. A woman emerged and appeared to be locking up. "Excuse me, but I have some pop for you."

She paused and smiled. "Oh, you must be the new teacher."

"Yes, I'm Jim Lang."

"Hi, Jim, I'm Jayne. I run the store. Actually I closed a couple of hours ago. I just was doing a little paper work…"

"I thought maybe the kids would want the pop."

She was unimpressed. "Oh, that! Thanks, but we still have lots here. I just thought you might as well bring that in since you were coming. We can get it tomorrow."

So much for playing the hero, I thought, as I rejoined the troupe on our front steps.

# Chapter Two

# The deal

"I think it's a lovely tie!" Mary objected, straightening the knot and eyeing me admiringly.

"But is it a 'teacher' tie? I mean, a Hereford bull's head with branding iron against red silk? For school?" I wasn't convinced.

"You look plenty teacher-like to me," she said firmly. "Now get into that school and start teachin'!"

I picked up my daily planner, its new pages sporting fresh scribbling that I hoped would pass as lessons for thirsty minds. I stepped out into the fresh fall air and headed for the rectangular, old school on the riverbank. The "sheer drop" Ron alluded to lay but twenty feet or so from the east side of the building. The new school, now nearing completion, was constructed of logs taken from the surrounding forest – as were all buildings in Nahanni Butte. This would be the third school building erected since formal education came to the settlement in the 1950's.

"Good morning, Laura!" My classroom assistant smiled nervously as I settled at my desk. Like most of the people in the village, Laura was striking, dark, raven-haired and painfully shy.

"Good morning, Mr. Lang."

"Who? Sorry, but of all the names I was called in the music business, 'mister' was not among them. Please call me Jim. The students can call me Mr. Lang, I suppose."

"Okay, Mr. Lang," she replied, then paused. "I don't think I can call you Jim, if that's okay." She blushed. "I like your tie."

"That's a relief. All my clothes are from the music business. I thought I'd spare the kids the Panama hat and white linen suit!"

"It's good to see you dressing up for school," Laura said. "Our last teacher didn't and I think the students need to feel they're in a regular school again."

"I agree. I plan to run this just like any school in the south. We'll raise the flag, sing 'O Canada' and raise our hands when we have a question. Sound good?"

"Sounds great!"

Twenty-seven kids showed up that day and somehow we all got through it alive. Laura and I organized them into grades, outfitted them with textbooks and got down to work. Over the days and weeks that followed, my old teaching skills resurfaced, were dusted off and put to use. I staggered home at the end of each day, exhausted, but satisfied that learning was taking place. We were beginning to feel at home.

The tranquillity and beauty of the north, the lush forests, sparkling mountains and majestic rivers worked their magic and slowly leached the southern toxins from our souls.

No doubt the Great Spirit thought one could get too much tranquillity. Perhaps a little noise might not be a bad thing. Perhaps that explained why airplanes appeared in the north. We were living in airplane heaven.

"I'm ho-ome!" Lunchtime! I burst into the kitchen to find two strangers at our table chowing down on what appeared to be my left-over roast beef sandwiches.

"This is Dave and, uh…" Mary started the introductions.

"Don…pleased to meet you. We really appreciate the lunch."

It seemed that they did the way they were plowing through it. Dave appeared to be the senior here, and Don the "new guy."

"Glad to meet you. I guess you brought in the Otter?"

"Yeah," Dave replied between bites, "we brought in some building supplies for Public Works. Got a furnace gun for you."

"Ron said he'd be sending one in. So, good flight?"

"So far," Dave answered. "Still have to hit Trout Lake and Wrigley today. Lots of time for the weather to screw us up, right Don?" The younger pilot just smiled.

I had been warned that pilots would tend to gravitate to the teacherage. I looked forward to it and our little home soon became a Fixed Base Operation for aviators of all stripes. They politely put up with my amateurish attempts at "hangar flying" while they tucked into soup and sandwiches.

There were white-knuckled newcomers – 300-hour recruits still unnerved from wrestling a bucking Cessna 185 in one of Nahanni's famous crosswinds. When the Chinooks blew down the Nahanni River valley, the crosswinds could make church-goers out of the crustiest atheists. They'd mumble about "making it back alive" and maybe rethink their career choices. Then there were the seasoned pros who would taxi Twin Otters into the village from the strip at a fast trot, clearing the trees on either side of the road by mere inches. With one propeller thrown into reverse thrust, they'd pivot on a dime, dusting off the eaves of the store on one side and the nursing station on the other without losing a wing-tip navigation light.

My interest in flying became a disease and as I pestered pilot after pilot for more juicy flying stories, it became apparent that my old excuse for not having my pilot's licence had lapsed. Up to now I could explain it away, saying I had money and no time, or I had time and no money. Although my salary as principal didn't come close to our earnings in the music business, it was steady and sufficient. Summer holidays provided the time and landlocked Nahanni Butte provided the all-important reason to fly. All I needed was a plane and a pilot's licence.

I didn't want to get into flying only to let my licence gather dust a few years later. I'd seen that happen to guys like me and you have to learn from the mistakes of others, it is said, for life is too short to make them all yourself. Every year thousands of intrepid Canadians earned their wings only to store them in mothballs shortly thereafter. If you really wanted to fly, you needed your own airplane and a good reason to fly it. We'd get the airplane first and then I'd get my licence in it. We'd save a lot of money that way. At least, that sounded good. I recited this argument a few times before trying it out on Mary. To my everlasting good fortune, I am blessed with a wonderfully understanding mate who had convinced herself of these simple facts even before I did. At two and a half, Johnny did not yet have a vote.

"So," I ventured to the same two pilots a few days later, catching Dave's eye between bites of a sandwich, "I figure it's time for me to get a plane and a licence."

"Uh, huh," Dave mumbled, smiling a little.

"So, I mean, what do you think? What kind of plane should I be looking for?"

"Depends."

"You mean on how much I want to spend?"

"Depends on a lot of things." He looked at me and smiled even more broadly. I wondered if I was being particularly stupid about this, or if there was some inside joke among pilots about guys like me. "If you're all going to fit in," he went on, indicating Mary, me and Johnny, who was chowing down a hot dog and paying us no attention whatever, "you're going to need a four-place. That probably means a Cessna 172."

"Yeah, a 172," I repeated. "That's pretty much what I'd figured. How much do they cost?"

"Depends." Another big smile. "Anywhere from not very much for not very much of a plane, to a whole lot for a whole lot of plane."

It was not the answer I'd hoped for. Don saw my confused look and decided to pipe up.

"It's really hard to say how much a plane will cost, Jim, even if it's a specific type, like a 172. It depends on the hours, how well they're maintained, what kind of panel it has."

"Panel?"

"Yeah, radios, avionics, and like that. They can cost more than a whole plane."

I looked at Mary, who was beginning to exhibit signs of aviation trepidation. I tried another tack. "Well, I know the 172 is pretty economical in terms of fuel consumption, right?"

"Jim," Dave swallowed and looked me square in the eye. "If the cost of fuel is going to make the difference for you, I'd suggest you forget the idea. The truth is an airplane is a big hole into which you throw vast quantities of cash. It's damn near impossible to justify owning one for economical reasons." Then he broke into a small smile, took a drink of coffee and added, "The only good reason to buy a plane is because you love flying and you love airplanes. If that's the case, nothing will talk you out of it no matter how logical the argument."

That settled it. Mary got up from the table and starting clearing the dishes. "God knows, he's nuts about flying and airplanes," she said. "If we don't do it now, I'll have to listen to him whine about it for the rest of my life," she leveled, then laughed. We all laughed.

Acquiring an aircraft poses challenges at the best of times and in the best of locations but attempting such a purchase with a home base at Nahanni required ingenuity, luck, and patience – mostly patience – and I had tons of it.

With nothing but time to lose, I decided to try first for the best possible deal, no matter how unlikely. We owned a large travel trailer for which we had no further use and required, as our research revealed, a Cessna 172. Our resolve firmed during the winter of 1985-'86. I let it be known through our rotating lunch guests that an even trade was sought: trailer for airplane. Months passed.

One day in early December an unearthly shriek startled us during lunch. Now, the radiophone is one bit of technology unhindered by progress. I had installed one in our living room shortly after moving in for reasons that seemed to make sense at the time. Radiophones don't ring, they scream.

I seized the monster, silencing its high-pitched squeal to take a call from Urs, who ran an air charter operation out of Fort Liard, 60 miles up the Liard River to the south. A distant Swiss-accented voice shouted through the warble and hiss.

"Yah, is zis Chim, over?"

"This is Jim Lang, Urs, over."

"Yah, say Chim, I sink maybe I haf a possible aircraft deal for you. Could you meet me in Fort Nelson soon, ofer?"

"I'd love to. Just say when, over."

Several "say agains" later we agreed to meet on my next trip to Fort Nelson, British Columbia.

In the meantime, I researched what I could about the airplane. I learned that the aircraft in question was a 1966 Cessna 172G and was parked in Fort Nelson, 150 miles to the south by air.

"What do you think?" I would ask assorted nonplused pilots around the lunch table.

"Could be good. Could be junk," they would reply, their obvious amusement a tad unnerving.

Hmmm, I thought, how do I get a straight answer about this thing? I had read every article written on 172s, although the first one generally said it all while the rest simply recycled the information: six-cylinder Continental engine, flat-spring landing gear, long nose gear, all bad or good, depending on who was talking. Having no direct experience, I was clearly at the mercy of the seller and of Urs.

Not yet thirty years old, Urs had already established himself as a legitimate competitor in the air charter business in southwestern NWT and BC. He pioneered the commercial use of the 172 as an economical people mover, an arguably dubious accomplishment. But his pride and joy was a Beaver on floats and he "chust luffed it."

He was a bear of a man, as his name suggests. Urs and his wife emigrated from Switzerland to build an aviation business in the last bastion of free enterprise, the Canadian North. Success didn't come easily, but he soon learned that the aviation commu-

24

nity was small and the smart operators learned to deal fairly with one another.

Urs dealt fairly with me. He and his pretty young wife extended their hospitality and their sofa when I arrived in Fort Nelson on a double-barreled mission: clinch the deal and take my pilot medical. It seemed Urs needed a trailer to use as a base of operations in Fort Nelson. He had inspected our Glendale Golden Falcon in Fort Simpson and was impressed. Unfortunately, without a plane to trade for it, he was like one hand clapping, as we used to say in the music business. So, he found me a plane. Applause! To the airport!

Urs and I crunched across the tarmac through the late winter snow, past rugged tail-wheel airplanes and low-wing speedsters and...there it was! Covered with snow and ice, and listing to one side, sat the object of my desire, C-FUPX. Fox-trot Uniform Papa X-Ray. Brown, white and a third color I usually associated with the rear end of a calf suffering from loose bowels, Papa X-Ray might not have impressed everyone as it did me. It is true that passion often blurs vision but in this, nature is being kind. Otherwise, the homely would never marry and airplanes like this beauty would languish on the ground indefinitely.

The left tire was flat. Wow, I thought, airplane tires go flat just like car tires. The truth was, in spite of my voracious interest, I still knew little about such details as tires, engines and the like. Urs cracked the door and I climbed into the pilot's seat. This was great! Look at all those dials and knobs.

"Vhy don't ve see if she'll start?" Urs suggested, injecting a necessary degree of practicality to counter my rose-colored euphoria. I slid over to the passenger seat to let the big man take over the magical task of firing up the engine. I was entranced as he pulled knobs and levers, checked this and that and then, somewhat anticlimactically, inserted an ordinary-looking key into the ignition and turned it.

Unlike Urs, I wasn't surprised in the least when the engine came to life. The prop was spinning around and the whole machine was shaking and shuddering like a dog excreting razorblades. Hunched in the cold cockpit, we vibrated in sync as the engine fought against the thick, cold oil and ingested frost from the cylinder walls.

"Oil pressure looks good," Urs commented cautiously as the shaking moderated. The engine slowly warmed up and smoothed to a delicious hum. Although he made every attempt to include me in his appraisal of the airplane, he was clearly satisfying himself that it was an airworthy craft. After all, my ignorance could not hide behind comments such as, "Oh, it has a carburetor, too?"

"I sink she's a good plane, zis vun sefenty-two, Chim," Urs pronounced after shutting her down. I watched the prop stop and shook myself, still utterly enchanted by the magic of it all.

"It sounds perfect to me," I cooed. "The only problem I see is the flat tire."

Urs laughed. "Ve'll take it for a good vorkout after zis deal is closed and she's carrying some insurance," he continued, "but I don't sink you could do much better zan zis, Chim."

UPX could have had three blown cylinders, a rotting airframe and fraying cables and I wouldn't have known the difference. I trusted Urs completely and he knew I was counting on his fair and careful assessment. I didn't know about airplanes but I knew an honest man when I met one and Urs was an honest man.

Later, back in town, I trudged up the hill to the medical clinic for my examination. I was still elated with the prospects of owning that 172. I suppose my heart would have been aflutter over a barn door or the Brooklyn Bridge if someone had told me they could fly and they'd take my trailer in trade. I secretly hoped my excitement wouldn't translate into an abnormally high blood-pressure reading, as I checked in at the doctor's office. At 38, this would be my last two-year medical. After I turned 40, it would become an annual event, sweaty palms and all.

I took a seat in the waiting room and tried to distract myself with a five-year-old copy of *Canadian Living*. Hmmm. "How to bake the perfect Sponge Cake." It wasn't working. I was too acutely aware of the fact that it could all end right here. More than a few sky-bound, would-be aviators were hauled abruptly back to earth, the victims of an unfriendly blood pressure arm-band.

"Mr. Lang?" It was my turn.

"Please be gentle. I spent ten years singing in bars!"

"This is the north, buddy," the gray-haired doctor laughed. "You'll have to do better than that to be unique!"

Shirt off, wires attached to my chest, I searched his face for clues as my heart battered away at the ECG machine. A few pokes, prods and one minor interrogation later, I was pronounced healthy enough to risk my life in aviation. I shouldn't have been so surprised. After all, I had met a number of active pilots, ten years older than me, who chomped cigars, swilled demon rum and still passed their medicals. I was a pretty clean liver by comparison.

Nevertheless, I was elated at clearing the medical hurdle. My pilot's licence was months away, but there was no point in buying a plane now if a bad ticker stopped me from flying it later. As I retraced my steps to Urs's apartment, I was walking on air – without a licence.

That evening, settled on Urs' sofa, I buried myself in manuals and books, eager to cram my brain with knowledge of airplane instruments, types and engines. Growing confident, I began to muse aloud about radar-altimeters and the merits of twin-engines versus singles. With fatherly patience, Urs eased me back to reality, offering advice I sometimes wish I'd taken more to heart over the years.

"You chust stay vis a vun sefenty-two," he said firmly. "She's not fast and she's not glamorous but at least you can afford to fly zuh sing. Zo many guys, zey buy some fancy airplane or zuh ozer and can't afford to fly zuh sing. Forget rrradar-altimeters," he chided, the "r" rumbling from deep in his chest, "up here, you chust don't fly ven you can't see zuh ground and if you can see zuh ground, you don't need no rrradar-altimeter."

Of course, I didn't know what I was talking about and he knew it but he couldn't afford to dampen my enthusiasm too much. After all, I was a key player in the deal. The elements of the deal, as it began to unfold, were interesting but not simple. Urs tried to explain them to me one more time.

"You vant a vun sefenty-two and Papa X-Ray is for sale, but I don't own it..."

"And you want my trailer but all you have to trade is…"

"Zuh crawler-tractor..."

"But the guy who owns the plane doesn't want a crawler-tractor, he wants a trailer?" I tried to grasp the increasing complexities of this proposed deal.

"Yah, but not your trailer. He vants anozer trailer, a different vun," he smiled.

To me, it looked hopeless: two trailers, a tractor and an airplane in a four-way trade with no cash involved. Henry Kissinger organized the peace deal with Vietnam but he'd be hard pressed to pull this one together. I was both elated and skeptical. A plane at last, but…

I tended to forget that this was the north, where, as Robert Service said, "strange deals are done under the midnight sun," or poetry to that effect. Before the weekend was out, I had signed on the dotted line at the bottom of a bill of sale unlike any other I, or

27

any of the co-signators, had ever seen. When the ink dried, the deal was done. I had traded my trailer to Urs, who traded his tractor and – the last minute deal-making detail – two pairs of snow-shoes to the owner of a fifth wheel travel trailer (not mine). He, in turn, traded said trailer to the owner of the 172, while I, in a state of shock and disbelief, handed my trailer over to Urs and took possession of C-FUPX, one of the prettiest 172s I had ever seen. Actually, it was one of the first 172s I had ever seen. Later the same day, I bought my first aircraft insurance policy and on Monday morning, Urs prepared to deliver me back to Nahanni in my own – my very own – airplane.

"Yow!" I shouted, as the seat dropped out from under my pants.

"She's got a nice clean stall," Urs commented over the roar in the cockpit. "Verrry nice," he said, his "r" merging with the engine, now in a full-power climb. I hung on to the hand-hold above my head and savored every moment. It flies! It really does fly!

For a half-hour we stalled, climbed, circled and cruised over the bush north of Fort Nelson until Urs was satisfied that Papa X-Ray was as sound as he'd hoped. I was just along for the ride, a wide-eyed puppy, grinning ear to ear.

"Okay," Urs yelled, "let's take her in, gas up and get you home."

We topped off the fuel up at the Esso dealer and blasted off for Nahanni Butte. I tried to study the panel, eager to learn the instruments but soon settled into a gentle, blissful passivity. I loved it all: the bush below, the Butte already visible far ahead and the hiss of the air rushing past my very own airframe. Urs sensed my emotions and quietly attended to the flying, smiling silently, no doubt remembering his own first plane.

"Johnny, look, our new plane!" Mary yelled as she ran across the hard-packed snow to UPX, moments after Urs killed the engine in front of the nursing station. Johnny trotted behind her, a blue bundle of snowsuit, scarf and red cheeks.

"Our plane?" he puffed. "This is our plane, mom?"

"Yes, it is," she said, squealing with excitement and giving him a hug as Urs tossed the cowl blanket over the engine compartment.

I sidled up to my little family. "What do you think?" I asked, proudly.

"It's beautiful! Can we have a ride?" She was almost jumping up and down now.

"Want a ride! Want a ride in the plane!" Johnny chimed in. Urs laughed.

"I kinda zought you might vant a ride," he said, pulling the cowl blanket off before it was completely on. "Chump in."

"You don't mind?" I asked. "I know you have to get back to Fort Nelson."

"Chim," he said, matter of factly, "your vife vants a ride in her plane. A lot of guys vould gif zer right arm for a vife like yours. Ve'll be right back."

I ran to the house, grabbed my camera and snapped pictures of them as they flew past the face of the butte, over the river and back down to the strip.

"Your plane, Jim?" Laura had wandered over to join me.

"Yeah, it is, Laura, what do you think?" I asked automatically, my eyes tracking UPX's progress up the road from the strip.

"It's a one seventy-two, eh?" she asked. Like everyone else in Nahanni Butte, Laura could identify planes as easily as most southerners could cars. "But, you don't have a pilot's licence, do you?"

"That's right," I turned to her. "In fact, we won't be seeing the plane again until the end of school, so take a good look."

"Never heard of anyone buying a plane before they got their pilot's licence," Laura said, laughing a little.

I hadn't thought that fact was so unusual up to that point. I watched Laura walk over to the store, then turned back to watch my taxiing plane and the beaming faces of Mary and Johnny. I walked over to help them out of the plane and for the first time the thought crossed my mind, what have I gotten myself into?

# Chapter Three

# BFC or bust!

The mosquitoes were getting worse. As the evening light of late June shifted northward, millions of these hungry pests rose in buzzing clouds from the forest and muskeg surrounding Nahanni Butte, mosquito capital of the world.

"He should be here by now, shouldn't he?" Mary asked, as we padded along the short trail from Greg William's outfitting lodge to our home in the settlement. I checked my watch, eight-thirty. Yeah, he should be here by now.

"There's no shortage of daylight so there's nothing to worry about. He'll be here soon," I answered, projecting more confidence than I felt. In fact, at this time of the year, pilots enjoyed twenty-four-hour daylight VFR – visual flight rules – in these parts. The sun wouldn't touch the horizon until after midnight. Even then it would just graze the crest of the spectacular four thousand-foot butte rising magnificently to the northeast across the placid Nahanni River.

It was a perfect evening for flying. Mary and I alternately swatted our attackers, glanced skyward and mused aloud about the adventure to come. Johnny padded alongside oblivious to both the mosquitoes and his parents' expectant chatter.

"Do you hear that?" I stopped walking.

"What, Dad?" Johnny eyed me curiously.

"Listen!" I hissed. "I think I hear a plane!" It was louder now. Three pairs of eyes searched the sky. Two pairs knew what they were looking for.

"That's a plane all right," Mary confirmed, craning her neck, hands shielding her eyes, "but where the heck is it?"

I hoped this was Papa X-Ray returning after five months absence to airlift the three of us out of Nahanni for the summer.

The unmistakable drone of an airplane merged with the incessant buzz of the insects. We scanned the azure evening sky, searching for the source. Funny, but this plane sounded different. It sounded so distant. Where the heck was it? The 185s, 206s, Twin Otters and Beavers usually roared in at circuit height out of the east from Fort Simpson or the south from Fort Liard. They usually didn't arrive overhead at nosebleed altitude.

"There he is!" I shouted, pointing almost straight up to a speck above our little family. "Boy, he's really coming in high."

I couldn't read the registration or even be certain it was a 172, but I knew this was C-FUPX. Apparently it was being piloted by the most cautious young man ever to venture into these parts.

Fresh out of Vancouver and armed with his new instructor's ticket, Bob Trerice, a shade younger than the twenty-two-year-old Cessna 172G Skyhawk, was taking no chances with our new baby.

I had secured Bob for the job by phone three weeks earlier. It took but one call to find a willing pilot who would fly Mary, Johnny and me to Brampton, Ontario, near Toronto in UPX where I was scheduled to take my pilot's licence. Eager to build hours, he had agreed. He was probably regretting that decision as he descended in a graceful spiral down to the tiny waving trio below.

A puff of dust marked the touchdown point on Runway 33. Captain Bob executed a perfect, gentle landing and coasted toward us. We were fairly jumping with anticipation at the far end. No doubt he was impressed with the mountain wall that rose up a few hundred yards off the north end of this interesting one-way strip. Like many northern airstrips, it evolved from an old mud trail, and that's not always the best way to design an airport. Dog-teams and trappers hadn't cared much about prevailing winds or worried about splatting into that mountain. That's why most folks elected to take off on Runway 15 and land on 33. Bob had already figured that out before he brought UPX to a stop a few feet from its proud owners.

We marveled at her sleek lines and rumbling engine, keeping a safe distance from the propeller we actually now owned. Full lean, throttle back, mags off, electric off, UPX shuddered and stopped. The surreal quiet of that pinpoint village enveloped us. I approached on the passenger side and opened the door – my door of my airplane! I loved the moment! A very relieved, dark-haired and handsome young man turned to greet me. I noticed his hand shaking slightly as he hung up the microphone.

"You must be Jim Lang." Did I hear him add, "The idiot who got me into this?" No. But there was something about his tone that implied it.

"Bob, it's good to see you!" I shook his hand. "How do you like the plane?"

He folded the Mines and Resources map, opened his door to step out and said, "Well, I've never flown a plane that was older than me before."

Yikes! Was he that young? "So, you're..."

"Just turned twenty," he finished for me, "and for awhile tonight I thought that might be as old as I'd ever get!"

"Why? What happened?" I expected the worst. Engine? Airframe? He planted his feet, rested one hand on the strut and explained.

"I've never flown outside greater Vancouver before. I just got my instructor's ticket and I really need to build hours because I've applied for the air force."

"Wow! The air force!" Mary piped up. "We should be in good hands, Johnny." She lifted him up and plunked his tiny bulk into the copilot's seat where he immediately began hauling on the yoke and making three-year-old noises.

"Well, I had no idea how much bush and water and rocks there was up here," Bob continued. "I got off the PWA jet in Fort Nelson, found my way to Northstar, where this plane was, and asked somebody how to get here. They threw me this Mines and Resources chart and said, 'Here, you can read charts can't you?' I'd never even seen a chart like that but I took off and holy cow! Hundreds of miles of bush! So I climbed nice and high."

"We noticed," I commented.

"Yeah, I wanted whatever safety I could get in altitude and, well, I found the place...but, whew! You people *live* up here?"

We all laughed, but Bob didn't laugh quite as hard as we did. "If you think you can handle it," I said, "taxi our baby here up into the village and..."

"Into the village?" Bob was skeptical. "You taxi right up into the village? I've never heard of such a thing!"

Again, I laughed but wondered for the first time if we'd have to supply a little of our own confidence for the coming trip.

"That's what we do up here, Bob. Really, it's okay. Just taxi it in and we won't have to haul all our stuff so far to load it." I paused. "We leave tomorrow morning. Do you think we'll make it?" I meant it as a joke.

"Well," he replied, flicking the master back on and measuring his words carefully, "we've got a chance, I guess." With that he restarted the engine and taxied in. We trailed behind, eating mosquitoes and dust kicked up by the prop wash.

As we settled Bob into our log house and got a hot tea into him, Bob and I silently concluded that, although arguably eccentric, neither of us was completely crazy to undertake the trip ahead. I approved of cautious pilots. They tended to live longer.

Bob had already planned the entire expedition to the last nautical mile. That evening he briefed me as we leaned over a half-dozen or more charts spread across our kitchen table and onto the floor. With precision the military would undoubtedly love, and which I could only assume was standard flight planning, he had highlighted our proposed route in pink and yellow stripes from Nahanni to Brampton. I was impressed. Bob was equally impressed by the size of our cargo that Mary was steadily piling up in the middle of the living room floor.

Our bathroom scale was pressed into service. Bob insisted we weigh baggage and crew. Mysterious slide rules flashed in his deft hands as he intently calculated weights, balances, temperatures and horsepower against the 2500 foot gravel strip from which we would launch the next morning. Running his fingers through his dark locks, he looked up to meet our admiring gaze. "We'll just make it," he announced with authority, then glanced down at his watch, noting it was almost midnight. "Let's get some sleep." He glanced out the window and was startled to see the school flag rippling in the breeze in broad daylight. "I don't believe this place," he muttered, packing up the charts and whiz-wheels. We closed the drapes to block the sun which was still struggling to set along the northern horizon and tried to get some sleep.

Mosquitoes never sleep. As we packed the plane the next morning, swarms of the bloodthirsty beasts seemed bent on giving us a proper send-off. A few of my students dropped by to say goodbye.

"Are you coming back again?" Stephen asked, his voice betraying some genuine and touching concern for his teacher.

"You betcha, Steve! You can't get rid of me that easy!" I roughed up his hair. "I'll be back in August with my new pilot's licence!"

"You're gonna be a pilot?" He seemed to imply that might be a stretch for a teacher.

"Yes he is, Steve," Mary answered, as she passed us carrying yet more bags and suitcases, "and he has to get going. Say goodbye to your mother for us and tell her we'll be back a couple of weeks before school starts, okay?"

"Okay, Mrs. Lang."

The little knot of children backed off as Bob fired up the engine from the right seat.

"Are you sure you can fly okay from that seat?" Mary asked, not caring one whit if she insulted Bob, the instructor. She had no intention of letting my position in the left seat undermine safety in any way.

"Actually, I probably have flown more from the right seat than the left in the last few months," Bob replied, with no hint of offense taken. On the other hand, I was offended.

"Now, Mary, we're not about to risk our lives just so I can pretend to be a pilot."

I was peeved. Bob insisted I take the left seat so I could practise flying on the trip. After all, why waste twenty-two hours of flying when I could be getting a leg up on my lessons next week? Nevertheless, I kept my hands to myself and my feet well clear of the rudder pedals as Bob taxied Papa X-Ray to the strip and lined up for takeoff. One more cabin check and then he called out, "Here we go!"

The growling little engine cared little for the precise planning of the night before. It just dug in and did its job with plenty of runway to spare. As Papa X-Ray blasted up into the brilliant morning sunshine, four happy faces looked down on the tiny village. Johnny instinctively waved goodbye. One mile gone; two thousand six hundred to go.

Nature was kind and prepared for us a beauteous batch of VFR. A boundless blue sky enveloped us, broken only by pastel puffs of cumulus clouds that marked our passage at speeds in excess of one hundred knots. To the north and west, snow-capped mountains hedged the horizon. To the south and east, the softer hills faded to distant flatlands.

I turned to check on Mary. Her brave smile said, "I'm fine – really!" but her ashen face and the sick bag clenched firmly in both fists told another story. At fifty-five-hundred feet over Pink Mountain, south of Fort Nelson, it was too late for the Gravol. Mary was learning an important lesson about cross-Canada travel in a Cessna 172. So was I. Johnny, asleep beside his mother in the back seat, was learning the art of unconscious aviating.

It was not yet noon and we were well into the second leg of our marathon journey. But the early summer sun stirred the atmospheric molecules and somewhere between Fort Nelson and Fort St. John the unstable air took its toll on the passengers.

Although my sole qualification was a burning desire to fly my new baby, Bob had allowed me to practise flying straight and level. However, judging by the effect of my flying abilities on my dear wife, I could only conclude that I was not the "natural" pilot I always thought I'd be. Then again, that's why we were here, VFR to Brampton - via Fort Nelson, Fort St. John, Grande Prairie, Edmonton, Calgary, Regina, Brandon, Kenora, Thunder Bay, Wawa, Sault Ste. Marie, and Wiarton - so that I could spend my summer holidays actually learning to fly UPX.

As we rounded the bend and Fort St. John appeared on the horizon, Mary's face began to reflect her assertion that she was, indeed, "fine – really." Johnny was still dozing.

Hey, this Bob-pilot guy was good! He greased it on at Fort St. John and just smiled that John Wayne "aw shucks" kinda smile when we ooohed and ahhhed. As for me, I had unofficially logged almost two hours of straight and level flight. The straight was slowly becoming straighter and the level was leveling off nicely, to the unspoken relief of my spouse. Not one to submit immediately to experts, Mary still wasn't sure I ought to be flying at all without a proper licence.

Next stop was Grande Prairie, Alberta, for fuel and then we were into the fourth leg to Edmonton.

"Should it be doing that?" I asked Bob, pointing to the guts of the compass lying motionless at an unusual angle within its shell.

Bob tapped it, examined it, and declared, "She's dead, Jim."

My stomach churned. Oh dear, I thought, here come the expenses everyone warned us about. I hadn't examined the instrument panel until now. After all, I didn't even know what most of the instruments were let alone whether they dated from this century or not.

"I've heard of 'barrel-type' directional gyros," Bob said, "but I've never actually seen one before. My dad, who's a senior pilot with Air Canada, once told me about Automatic Direction Finders that looked like that." He went on, giving the black box a poke. "Until now I didn't know whether or not to believe him."

In spite of Bob's electronic snobbery, the black, dented Cessna-ARC brand radio seemed to work flawlessly – on all ninety channels – and as we approached Edmonton Municipal we were grateful for the radar transponder retrofit some previous owner contributed to UPX.

Droning across the prairie flatlands, we entertained ourselves by reading Papa X-Ray's log book. With 5,500 hours on the bottom line, this little Skyhawk had been around some. It had carried students and instructors at Whitehorse and Kelowna and had serviced drilling rigs in the Northwest Territories. Five thousand dutiful hours showed in the book. She wasn't old, I reasoned, she was experienced. She had been everywhere, done everything and never let anyone down. That was good enough for me even if it left Bob less than enthusiastic.

I turned back to yell at Mary, "She flies a lot better than the travel trailer, hey?" Mary didn't answer, but her face said it all. Johnny was asleep, his head resting on her shoulder. She was loving this.

We floated down over Edmonton, a former home in a former life and set down like a feather at the Municipal Airport, Edmonton's crown jewel. As we taxied in, I wondered which would still be around in twenty years, Papa X-Ray or the much maligned Muni Airport? The Muni was a national treasure, rich in aviation history and a short cab ride to downtown. An unbeatable one-two punch. Yet NIMBYs threatened both with extinction. How come everyone didn't love aviation as much as I did? Why was I infected with this bug?

Directly across the street from the Muni, an avionics shop charged me fifty dollars for a rebuilt compass. "Cheap at twice the price," I mused to myself as we screwed it onto the dash. Surely the deities protect the ignorant and innocent for it was the only money I spent on that panel in the three years I owned UPX.

Our rapture grew with each passing hour. Canada from 3,500 feet was unlike any perspective we had experienced in our years of criss-crossing North America by road and jet. It was a living map moving below us. So that's how the Saskatchewan River is routed through Edmonton. Look how shallow these prairie lakes appear. Why are we still over that lake?

"Why are we still over that lake?" Mary tapped me on the back, urgently. "We're not moving, Jim!"

"Headwind!" I yelled back, then looked over at Bob.

"Headwind," he confirmed. Somewhere west of Medicine Hat we learned about the effect of headwind on ground speed as it interfaced with a 172 powered by 145 anemic horses. The lesson was embellished by the effect of the same wind on the same aircraft when blowing across the runway at Medicine Hat, Alberta.

"Why are we landing sideways?" Mary wanted to know, then added, "Oh, I see!" as Bob floored the left rudder pedal and set Papa X-Ray down straight, battling a series of jarring buffets and gusts.

"Interesting," Bob breathed as we lurched through the final rollout before turning off to the pumps.

"By God, it's old UPX!" the elderly gentleman exclaimed as he strolled out to top off the tanks. "I instructed in this plane twenty years ago. 'Course, she was painted maroon and white then and pretty as a bug."

I was transfixed. He actually knew this very plane, my very plane! Our very own plane, as Mary would put it.

"Sure, there were two of them - sisters, UPX and UP something else."

Well, how do you like that? I thought. She's famous!

And kind of slow, we discovered as we headed back into the wind toward Regina, Saskatchewan, our stop for the night. "Seventy's not a good ground-speed, Bob?" I asked as we tracked the Trans-Canada past Moose Jaw.

"Not even when it's knots, which it's not," he yawned.

A soggy west-coast boy, Bob was uncomfortable on the prairies but it was home to me. He rustled the charts and studied frequencies, desperate to figure out where we were. "God!" he snorted, "How the heck can you navigate out here. There are virtually no surface features to use as a reference. In BC we have mountains, lakes..."

"Just drop this sucker down to 500 feet and hand me the binoculars." Bob did as I suggested. I scanned the next town. "Pense," I announced.

"How the heck did you do that?"

"Have a look. The name of every town is painted in ten foot letters on the grain elevators."

He took a look. "Well, whaddaya know!"

"I might not know much about flying but I know the prairies," I stated flatly.

At Pense you're practically on a long final for Runway 07 at Regina, a special stop for the three of us. I grew up on a farm north of there, near Raymore. When Mom and Dad retired they moved into the Queen City.

My dad tried to make intelligent conversation about our new plane as they helped us carry the luggage from Guy's Regina Airport Esso to their waiting car. Although he was genuinely interested, he knew more about tractors than planes.

That evening, after Mom's award-winning perogies, sausages and home-made Saskatoon pie, Bob helped me write up a pre-flight checklist for the plane. Dad listened in and couldn't help piping up when he heard Bob mention the "mag check."

"Mag check?" he retorted, "Do you mean magneto?"

"Yup," I replied confidently, relieved that he'd chosen an engine part I actually knew something about. So did he, it seemed.

"Good heavens, man, we had magnetos on the John Deere tractor forty years ago! Surely the engine's newer than that!"

"Actually, not much," I admitted, weakly.

I needn't have worried. Dad thought John Deeres were the best tractors ever built. His respect for Papa X-Ray grew considerably. Still, he smiled quietly to himself, amused and amazed that airplanes and farm tractors could have anything whatsoever in common. He shook his head and chuckled, "Magnetos."

Well, if we were happy, they were happy for us. Mom and Dad waved and watched as we departed Regina International for Brandon, Manitoba, and points east into a headwind that had overstayed its welcome where we had not.

And that was part of the reason Brandon didn't answer at first when we radioed in about ten miles out. Bob and I examined the triangular airfield when we approached within two miles. "Funny, I thought Brandon was bigger than this," I observed.

"You've been here before?" Bob asked.

"Sure, lots of times, but never by Cessna. Brandon is a city, by prairie standards, and it should take up some space down there somewhere!" I speculated.

"Uniform Papa X-Ray, Brandon." The old ARC radio came to life via the cockpit speaker. Bob picked up the hand mike.

"Uniform Papa, X-Ray, Brandon, go ahead."

"UPX, you say you are approaching Brandon, over?"

"Affirmative."

"Papa X-Ray, describe the airfield, over," came the request.

"Roger that," Bob transmitted, "we see a triangular field...with, umm," he paused, as a bad feeling started welling up inside us simultaneously. He stopped transmitting and said to me, "With white X's on each threshold of the runway!"

The ARC crackled. "Papa X-Ray, you are at Rivers Airbase, an abandoned airfield. *Do not land, repeat, do not land!*" The instruction was firm, but there was something in its delivery that led me to believe we were not the first to make that mistake.

We banked left, blushed bright red and ten minutes later Brandon appeared right where it should have been – just a bit later than we expected.

The next day, Manitoba disappeared in the rear-view mirror. (Yes, Papa X-Ray had a rear-view mirror. No, I didn't know why it needed a rear-view mirror.) Ahead, Northern Ontario appeared on the horizon. New terrain: rocks and bush…hmmm. Just like the north, only farther south. New weather: rain. And new lessons to be learned: time to spare, travel by air. Don't fly anywhere you can't get back from by bus. VFR? Vait For Rain. Lesson number, what was it now, three? Meteorology: The worst weather always happens over the least hospitable terrain at the most inconvenient times with the closest airport near the most expensive motels. Spell that Kenora, Ontario.

Lesson number four: Special VFR arrivals will wait until all corporate jet departures have read back their IFR – instrument flight rules – clearances three times each or until the ceiling hits the bush, or both. Bob was furious.

"Kenora radio, Uniform Papa X-Ray requesting special, holding over lake at 800 feet, over!"

"Papa X-Ray stand by, departing traffic."

"I've never seen so many towers and so many floatplanes in one place!" Bob exclaimed, slamming the microphone back into its slot. The rain continued and the ceiling threatened for what seemed an eternity.

"Papa X-Ray, special VFR approved, report established on final."

"Finally!" Bob retorted, "Those guys are departing into the safety of IFR while we have to risk our lives out here waiting for them to leave! I wish those government guys would remember who is safe in the chair and who is up in the air!"

It wasn't like Bob to get upset, so Mary and I kept quiet until we were safely on the ground. Never argue with the guy who holds your life in his hands, I say.

We checked into a motel (high season, rates to match), rented some movies and settled in for the duration.

"What's a lubber-line?" I asked Bob, lounging on the bed, watching Dan Aykroyd's *Trading Places* for the third time. I had been studying the *From the Ground Up* text book and was determined to show off my growing technical vocabulary.

39

"Don't know. Don't care," he responded, his gaze wandering blankly out the window to the leaden skies beyond.

Two days of take-out chicken later, we bolted for a blue hole in the Ontario sky and made Thunder Bay by evening. But we lost Bob.

We didn't lose him forever, of course, or even for the rest of the trip. Bob's father had phoned with the news the night before. Bob had been accepted as pilot-trainee by the Canadian Armed Forces. He was beside himself with surprise and delight.

"I can't believe they took me!" he yelled, pumped with excitement.

"Wow! Congratulations! Next time you visit Kenora, you can buzz the field in an F-18."

We all laughed. Mary and I were happy for him but not in the least surprised. One look at Bob, one conversation with Bob and you knew he was air force material. More than once I had almost saluted him, just out of instinct.

"Are you going to fly jets?" Johnny asked.

"Did you say, 'Are you going to fly jets?'" Bob asked slowly, dropping to a crouch in front of Johnny.

"Yeah. Are you going to fly jets?" Johnny asked again.

"Yes, yes I am! I mean, I hope to!" Bob replied, then stood up and turned to Mary and me. "I understood him," he said, sounding amazed.

"You mean, you…" Mary began

"…never understood a thing the kid said until today." Bob answered her question before she could finish it.

I laughed. Of course, we'd assumed everyone understood Johnny and Bob had never indicated otherwise. Mind you, he hadn't talked to Johnny much now that we thought about it.

"Well, there you go," I added my two-bits worth, "if you can talk to and understand a three-year-old, you're going to be perfect for the military!"

Bob laughed. We were going to miss him when our trip was over.

It was over too soon. A breath-taking flight around Lake Superior, a jump across Manitoulin Island and the emerald waters of Lake Huron, a quick fuel stop at Wiarton and the checkerboard farmland of the Ontario heartland opened up below us. Twenty-one hours and forty minutes flying time from lift-off at Nahanni Butte, the Caledon Hills disappeared below us and the orange rooftops of the Brampton Flying Club appeared through the summer haze ahead. Time to set the ARC at 123.4.

"Brampton Unicom, Uniform Papa X-Ray, over."

"Uniform, Papa, X-Ray, Brampton, go ahead."

"Brampton Unicom, Uniform Papa X-Ray, Cessna 172 three miles north at two thousand four hundred, VFR out of Wiarton, landing Brampton, advisory please."

"Uniform Papa X-Ray, Brampton altimeter two niner niner niner, we are active on two six and there are several in the area."

"Papa X-Ray, thank you, Brampton."

Bob banked Papa X-Ray into final for Runway 26. "Holy cow, are these runways ever narrow! You're going to have fun here, Jimmy boy!" he laughed as he set us down and taxied up to the gas pump circle near the door of the club.

UPX got lighter and lighter as the pile of luggage, pizza boxes and toy bags grew around Johnnny, who sucked on a chocolate milk in the middle of the lobby. Not surprisingly, people were beginning to notice us.

"You must be Jim Lang," a be-suited executive-type mused, stepping forward and extending his hand.

"How'd you know?" I asked, mildly surprised, taking the firm grip.

"Says 'Simpson Air' on your cap and I'm not expecting anyone else from Nahanni Butte this week," he smiled. "I'm Rick Wynott, welcome to the flying club. You wrote me a few months back, saying you would like to take your pilot's licence."

"Right and right again," I replied. "You see that plane out there?" I pointed to Papa X-Ray. "Well, I own that beauty and it's the only transportation we've got to get us back to Nahanni Butte. So, you see, I kinda need a licence in a pretty big way. How long does it take to finish the course?"

"The accelerated version can be done in fifteen weeks," he responded, smiling. "How much time do you have?"

"Five weeks."

"Well, I guess we'd better get started," he replied, not missing a beat.

41

# Chapter Four

# Wings

"What are you doing?" I asked through the roar and rattle of UPX in full climb. I had misread this guy completely.

"Teaching you how to fly," he responded evenly while he calmly attached circular soap-dish pads to every instrument in the panel. He's a madman, I realized. I was concerned but not yet in full panic.

"Now," he continued, "let's see a climbing turn to two seven zero degrees. Level off at thirty-five hundred feet."

"But," I started to protest, "I don't have any instruments!"

"You've got your compass and altimeter. Now just look through the windshield and fly the airplane."

This was not what I had expected at all. I looked at him, suddenly noticing how much he resembled Hitler. The torture continued until I was reduced to a pile of white knuckles shot through with pure adrenaline.

Just yesterday I was shaking hands with Rick Wynott. "You're taking on a lot of hard work in a short time, Jim," he'd said, fixing me with a serious look. Rick didn't say it was impossible, but he wanted me to understand that earning my licence in five weeks would not be a stroll in the park.

"Well, I've already read a few ground school books and I have nothing else booked except working on getting my ticket," I replied confidently. "Besides, I have to be back in the classroom in Nahanni Butte in eight weeks. I need to allow enough time to take the written exam and then fly back north." I recited the logic behind the predicament I'd created for myself.

Rick was understandably skeptical but he set to work immediately. The Brampton Flying Club is one of the largest, most respected flying schools in the country and although they discouraged attempts like mine to earn "quickie" licences, they tried hard to accommodate the needs of their customers no matter how bizarre.

A slender, dark-haired, young man sauntered up, smiling behind a Clark Gable mustache. I made a mental note: This guy is not a day past half my age.

"Jim, meet Doug Hannah." Rick introduced us right there in the lobby. "Doug, Jim needs his licence in five weeks, so I guess you'd better get started."

"Well, we can try," he replied, wryly giving me the quick once-over. "How about tomorrow morning, seven sharp?"

"Done." We shook on it. Let the games begin.

I had forty-five flying hours to go and five weeks to fly them off. Easy to say, not so easy to do. I had zipped up my new black leather jacket, hopped onto the hot leather seat and kick-started my borrowed Honda 360T. Brother-in-law Rod had loaned me his immaculate cherry red motorcycle so I could commute from the flying club to Brampton and back. Fifteen minutes later, I rumbled up the driveway, settled into my mother-in-law's comfortable double side-split on Bartley Bull Parkway and pondered my fate. Mary and her mom, Olive, had driven up to the cottage on Georgian Bay with Johnny, ninety miles north of the airspace I was about to terrorize. The house was all mine.

I had plunked down on the sofa, taken a bite out of a Wendy burger and flipped open the crisp new cover of the *Cessna Private Pilot Manual*. Hmmm. This is a thick book – a lot thicker than *From the Ground Up*. A twinge of fear shot through me. I calmed myself. I wasn't going to need fifteen weeks like those other poor jerks. I was going to be one of those naturals we all heard about. I loved airplanes. I'd read thousands of flying magazines. I'd spent hours talking the ears off pilots. I will take to aviating like a frog to a mud puddle. Just give me a chance. No fear of flying here. My faith in Bernoulli and Continental was unshakable. Navigating? Piece of cake! Heck, we found our way here, 22 hours VFR from Nahanni Butte, didn't we? Of course the "we" included Bob, a licenced, instructor-rated pilot - but, hey! How hard can this be? I mean, really.

"Use your feet. You're not driving a car."

His tone was firm, clear and instructional. Not a hint of panic or terror, or any indication that his life was passing before his eyes. Clearly Doug Hannah, world's calmest flying instructor, was oblivious to the specter of imminent death at the hands of his newest student pilot.

Sighting through the splattered intestines of a large greenish bug, I noted that my touchdown target point, a projection of my approach path, would be just to the right of the decimal point in the 123.4 painted in large letters on the roof of the Brampton Flying Club. There I was, facing certain death, wrestling a bucking, porpoising Cessna 172 away from the roof of the flying club by dint of brute force and psychic energy, only to point it at the turf on the other side of the strip. And my instructor? Oblivious. Surely he would take the controls any second now and save us, right? He must be paralyzed with fear, I thought, frantically. Why doesn't he grab the controls and save our lives?

"Watch your airspeed, Jim." He was inspecting his fingernails! Watch my airspeed? Right, he had removed the soap-dish pads before entering the circuit so I glanced at the airspeed indicator. Holy cow! I hit full power. The nose lurched up and pointed to the pearly gates. Dear God! Did I hear a response? *"Yes, my son? I'd help you but you're the one who wanted to fly. I merely save souls."*

"That's good. Now ease it off a bit." Did this guy have a pulse? I screamed at him silently. This aircraft is out of control! This pilot is also out of control! Yet, as the asphalt raced up to meet us, his tone was calmly surreal, as if he were guiding me into a parking spot at K-Mart. But wait! What's this? That's a runway appearing under me. This is asphalt, not grass or trees or the flying club roof! Wait for it…yes! The wheels touched, mains first!

"Hold the nose up, it's not over yet," Doug admonished.

How did he do that? I wondered. I could see him out of the corner of my eye just smiling that placid smile. He didn't land the airplane at all, I did. How did I do that?

And so passed the first few days of managed terror and soaring exhilaration. Flying was tough enough but there was still ground school to master. Hours in the chair were added to hours in the air.

I was staring at the picture of the landing aircraft on the microfilm screen. There appeared to be two aircraft…wait, no, my eyes are crossing with fatigue. I gathered up my books and headed for the Honda. Good old Rod! I was really starting to enjoy motorcycling again, thanks to his generosity. Leaning into the turn, I cut the corner past the BFC sign "Learn to Fly", shifted down and twisted the throttle. Rod knew what I was going through. Mary's brother had taken his licence years ago. In those days the Brampton Flying Club occupied the site where the OPP now trains recruits, on the eastern edge of the city. No asphalt back then, he'd said, just grass – and mud when it rained. I wondered if it was easier to land on turf. Anything would be an improvement over the controlled crashes that had passed for my first few landings.

The cool evening air revived me as I putted down the back roads to Brampton. What a great family I'd married into. Other, more timid in-laws might have questioned the sanity of a middle-aged man riding motorcycles and flying "tiny" airplanes when he should be have been mowing the lawn and drinking beer. Olive could have shunned me, instead she calmly broke all the rules for mother-in-lawhood. She even called the BFC to help make arrangements for me while I was still in Nahanni. I'd suggest perhaps she had sinister motives for encouraging me to take up flying, but the fact that I was to carry her daughter and grandchild aloft put that thought to rest.

Olive. Kind, funny and generous, was more of a friend than mother-in-law. While she and my little family browned themselves at the beach, tossing back cool drinks and barbecuing steaks, I pulled the Honda up to Wendy's for another "old-fashioned" burger. A few minutes later, I stumbled through the door at Bartley Bull, wolfed the food, then crawled up the steps to my bedroom and fell into bed, exhausted.

Eyes closed, my body on autopilot, I lay prone, wondering if I had bitten off more than I could chew. It was now apparent that I was not a "natural" pilot. I mulled the hard truth: I was a middle-aged man with middle-aged reflexes who hadn't taken any kind of formal examination in more than twenty years. What if I don't make it? What if...?

"You've just received a weather briefing," Doug said the next day. "Your destination is below VFR; you must divert to Mansfield." That calm instructor's voice again. Twenty-five hundred feet above the green patchwork quilt of rural Ontario, Papa X-Ray bucked and twisted in the thermals like a spooked bronco. Today's lessons: diversions. More like perversions, to my way of thinking. And Mansfield, yet. That's three times this week I've had to find Mansfield. I scanned the horizon. How do they manage to hide a whole airport like that? I turned the chart right side up with one flailing hand while the other struggled with the yoke. Another quick look out the window and then at the chart. Okay, I thought, we're here, right? Right. And we have to go there, so draw a line from here to...

"Watch your altitude." Oops. Right. Fly the airplane. No matter what, just remember to fly the airplane. Okay, we're here.

45

Quick look. No, we're not here anymore. We're...where the heck are we anyhow? A pleading look to the perpetually smiling Doug. No dice. He was happily enjoying the view and clearly ready to let me burn fuel until I figured it out.

It had to be down there! This was that road and that was this hydro line and for pity's sake it had to be right down there! I had been flying the same triangle for twenty minutes. Mansfield! Why can't I find the place? Sure it's a green airstrip on a green field in a green township but everyone else finds it, don't they?

"Not usually, actually," Doug admitted. I realized I must have been thinking out loud. He was smiling at me as he pointed a finger straight down. There it was. We were less than a quarter mile south of it the whole time and it was in sight the whole time and Doug saw it the whole time. But I didn't, and that's the whole point. Navigation was not turning out to be a piece of cookie, as the one Swiss student would say.

We joined the Brothers Swiss for lunch. They weren't actually brothers but they were Swiss and they were my psychological edge. They were my comfort and solace in my near despair at not soloing in ten hours, or twelve. They had but four weeks to finish the course. Four weeks! And they came all the way from Switzerland with return tickets already bought. And they were actually doing it.

"You soloed?" I dropped, casually.

"Yes, today," the older one said with visible relief. "You?"

"Not yet," I answered quietly, almost under my breath.

Rick Schobesberger, I'll never forget that name. Not like mild-mannered Doug, no, not Rick. Class One instructor, Rick was. Until he or someone very much like him said so, it was no go solo.

"Watch your airspeed!" Rick barked. "You're way too slow! And quit steering this thing like a car! This isn't a car, it's an airplane and you're off by fifty feet on your approach. Do you know how much fifty feet is? It's higher than the clubhouse! Use your feet, your feet!"

My pre-solo flight wasn't going well at all. I could do better. This guy just gets me all nervous and then I do bad landings and then I don't get to solo. This isn't going well at all, I thought, as I slammed onto Runway 26, cleared the active and braced for another torturous circuit.

"Pull over," Rick commanded. "Stop. Now, listen. Watch your airspeed. Goodbye." And with that he got out of the airplane.

"What do you mean, goodbye?" I asked. I was as puzzled as I was fried.

"Go do it. You'll do fine." Then he smiled and waved me on. Slowly the full force of what he had said hit me. He wants me to solo. Well, at last! You bet I'll solo and solo I did. Clearly there was more than a modicum of method in Rick Schobesberger's madness.

It was over before it started and there was nothing to it. Only after I rolled to a stop on the taxiway did the exhilaration wash through me. Perspiration washed through as well, it seemed, as I noticed my soaked armpits. Yahoo! I shouted and taxied proudly to the pumps.

Rick casually shook my hand as I entered the club. "Do you always taxi with your flaps down and your landing lights on?" he asked with feigned sarcasm. Then he jerked my shirt tail from my pants, produced a hidden pair of scissors and in a quick motion snipped off a chunk of my brand-new BFC golf jersey. The rites of passage. What a great day! Gotta call the relatives and give them the great news.

"I soloed today," I announced cheerfully over the phone to Mary, who was shivering in a phone booth 90 miles to the north on Georgian Bay.

"That's nice, dear," she responded with not quite the adulation I had expected. But then she had always assumed I would get my licence so just go ahead and get it, right? Right.

Four weeks down, one to go. London, Ontario, my solo cross-country...

"Uniform Papa X-Ray cleared for takeoff and note the lay on rollout!" London Tower crackled.

This was my last cross-country. I'd made it to London with no problem. Now, I just had to get back to Brampton. Note the lay on rollout. What the heck did that mean? I rolled out onto the numbers. If you're not sure you'd better not go, I thought, and abruptly stopped on the runway.

"Uniform Papa X-Ray! Cleared takeoff! *No delay* on rollout! *Get going, I have landing traffic!*"

Oh, "*no de-lay*", that's what he meant. The cabin glowed night-light red, a reflection of my burning face as I realized my error. "Papa X-Ray," I responded, "sorry about that."

Papa X-Ray had grown forty hours older since the beginning of this course and I had a few more gray hairs showing on my temples. Finally, this was it. Not really it, not the actual flight test mind you but the last training flight before the flight test and for me it was almost as important.

"Pass this," Doug had said, "and the actual test is a snap."

I hadn't passed the last preflight test so this one was critical. The written test was booked for August 1 and the flight test would have to be done by then. I had done solo spins and stalls, my solo cross-country and lots and lots of solo circuits. And I had screwed up plenty. But today would be perfect. I would divert to Mansfield or Hare field as if on a guide wire. I would spin like a falling leaf and I would land like...

"There's a bit of a crosswind; you might not want full flap...oh, you do...well, okay." Doug was his usual agreeable self. But, hey, this was supposed to be a short-field landing over an obstacle and by George I was going to nail it. The landing, that is, not the heavy equipment working to the right of the runway which is where the nose now pointed.

"Whoa, baby!" I coaxed, kicking the rudder to the stops. Straight at last but wait, we're dropping like a rock. Airspeed! Airspeed! Full power, balloon up, settle down, twist sideways, straighten out and drop like a rock. Oohmph! Bounce and bounce again and...

"Hold the nose up. It's not over yet."

Why does he always have to remind me? And how can he be so calm? The flight test has to be this week or never. We stopped. Avionics off. Mags off. Electrics off. Doug turned to me.

"You know, Jim," he began thoughtfully, "I honestly believe that was the worst landing you ever made." I had to agree. It was a stinker.

"But," he went on, "there's no reason you won't do better on the test on Friday." Gulp.

The big day. It was all over. We were sitting in UPX on the ramp after the flight test. Rick Wynott sat in the right seat checking off boxes on his sheet, noting this and noting that. My mind raced. Good heavens, man, tell me I failed! It's obvious I must have failed. That last landing was almost as bad as the worst I've ever done. And the simulated forced approach, well, it was okay but embarrassing.

The flight test. I played it again, mentally. We'd finished just about everything else so when Rick pulled the power off and announced an engine failure, I wasn't too surprised. Not as surprised as I was when he asked me to do one spin to the left and come out on the same heading. I had hauled it up to a stall, kicked left rudder and held the yoke to my beating heart. That sickening nose-over and then the free-fall of a spin. I have no idea what heading I'm on now, I thought. I barely know which way is up. Well, what the heck, I'll act like I know what I'm doing, sometimes that works. Neutral yoke, opposite rudder, power on and...I can't believe it. I nailed it to within five degrees. Okay, there is a God.

But now it was simulated forced approach time. I rattled off the routine: best rate of glide, look for a field... I like baled fields, myself. I've been a farmer and I know that those fields are firmly packed. All you have to do is miss the bales of hay. But most people, especially designated flight examiners, prefer pastures. Hey! There was a pasture right below us! Actually, it looked like about a ten-acre field next to a nice farmhouse. I set up my approach, finishing with "crack doors," and, just as I was sure I would make the field, he called, "Overshoot," and turned to his notes.

"I think you would have made the field," he commented. That was unusual because he hadn't commented on much, "but that grass in there is three feet high and there's another two feet of water underneath it."

"How do you know that?" I asked, amazed that he knew.

"Because that was my house and my yard," he answered, clearly delighted with himself. He must have pulled that stunt before but it was the first and only time I'd heard it.

He's still writing! Stop that writing and for pity's sake, say something, I thought.

He must have read my mind – or had I said that out loud?

"Oh, you passed all right," he looked up, casually, "mind you, I've seen better short-field landings." He turned back to his paperwork, smiling, "I just have to finish filling out these forms."

The relief was palpable...almost too much to absorb. I celebrated for about five minutes before I remembered: The written exam. Tomorrow.

Six sweating "waitlings" sat nervously around a coffee table at the Department of Transport office. The three-hour exam was over. I had used the entire three hours and perhaps a few seconds more, handed it in and sat down to wait. I was wound up tighter 'n a backlash at a fishing derby.

"What'd you put for that cross-country question on ETA?" One waitling asked another. Why do we do this? I thought. It's torture. It's over. The paper is in the computer never more to be touched by human hands. Even now it's a done deal.

"Thirty-two minutes, right?" the second waitling replied, hopefully. Thirty two minutes! That can't be right! Can it? That's not what I calculated! My mind reeled.

"That's what I got, too!" another waitling burbled, his voice drenched in relief. The woman at the desk called a name. Not my name but, yes, that guy's name. He jumped up and ran to the counter.

"Congratulations, sixty-eight per cent, a pass. You should study these questions for your own future reference." Another name. Another pass. Seventy-six per cent. Wow! And he's the guy who got a different answer for the navigation question than I did. This was bad, really bad. The third, fourth and fifth names were called. All passed. This was a conspiracy. Those guys set me up. I just knew it. Right now if someone offered me the lowest passing mark, the bare minimum in place of my actual mark, I'd have grabbed it like a game show contestant on Benzedrine.

"Mr. Lang?" This was it. She was smiling. Was this some cruel trick? She was playing with me, sure she was. "Last but not least, we hope," she added mischievously. How could she have said that? This really was it, the last chance. I'd have to wait 30 days to rewrite this test if I failed. I didn't have a month. In 30 days I would be back in front of a classroom of eager faces in Nahanni Butte, all wanting to know why my airplane was still in Brampton, wherever that was, and why didn't I get my licence?

"Eighty-six per cent," she said smiling, "best mark of the day. Now, if you'll..."

I didn't hear the rest.

# Chapter Five

# North by northwest

"Here, let me carry some of those," Olive offered, stepping spryly past the peek-a-boo headlights on the front of her '77 Dodge. Her smile flashed in the late afternoon sunshine as she began hauling boxes across the Brampton Flying Club parking lot. She'd parked near the plane which I had tied down on the ramp near the fence.

"You don't have to, Mom!" Mary protested but clearly she had her hands full with Johnny and the daunting pile of cargo waiting to be loaded into Papa X-Ray's bowels.

Olive toted a load of baggage bulging with Mary's summer purchases ("Jim, we can't beat these prices up north!") through the gate to the tarmac beside UPX. A strong Irish-Canadian woman who had spent much of her life on the farm, she barely broke a sweat from such "easy" work. As we prepared for the flight, I expected her to look, act and sound worried but her face betrayed only a hint of concern.

She was a rare breed, Olive, an understanding and trusting mother-in-law. If her daughter was prepared to risk life and limb aboard this "tiny" aluminum kite then it was apparently quite all right with her. The fact that she would allow us to risk the limb and life of her grandson underscored her cool and non-judgmental nature. The young heir to our debts trundled across the pavement, alternately shaping and reshaping Blaster, his favorite Transformer toy.

Olive set the bags down beside Papa X-Ray and went back for another load as if she were seeing us off on the old CPR Transcontinental. No matter that the pilot boasted a scant fifty-eight hours total time in his log book. No matter that the trip would cover thousands of miles between Brampton and Nahanni Butte. Nor did she seem concerned that much of the journey would be over inhospitable moose pasture. Olive, bless her heart, was cool.

Meanwhile, Mary, my wife, the third child and second daughter of my mother-in-law, busied herself with loading our Skyhawk. No cranny was left unplugged. I supervised weight and balance, easily the most difficult of the tasks. Yes sir, we might be at gross weight but, by Bernoulli, our weight would be balanced.

I had learned many shiny new skills in my compressed five-week training period. The crisp, new private pilot licence testified as much to the BFC's fine training program as it did to my diligence. Whatever else Doug Hannah had accomplished with his middle-aged student, he managed to instill equal parts confidence and caution. While I wasn't the least bit fearful about the looming flight, I was diligent to a fault.

"Not in there," I chided Mary. She was attempting to cram a VCR into the rear compartment. "That has to go in the back seat. It's too heavy for the rear baggage area."

"All right, all right!" she said, doing a slow burn in response to my "commanding officer" inflections.

Young son Johnny, tanned a golden brown from a summer cavorting on the beach at Georgian Bay, squeezed his body into the car-seat we'd pressed into service as "plane-seat." He promptly set about organizing his cramped space so that he could best access his Transformers which would distract him for most of the trip. God bless those toy-makers, every one.

"When are we going to get back to Nahanni Butte, Dad?" he asked, the first of what would be seven hundred such questions. I leaned in and strapped him firmly into place.

"Well, it all depends on the weather," I answered carefully, taking my skills as a pilot as given. "Are you sure you don't have to go to the bathroom?"

A final hug, an isolated tear or two and we got down to the business at hand. Olive waited to see the takeoff, perhaps not willing to believe we would actually be undertaking this trip until she personally witnessed our rotating beacon blink and fade into the afternoon sky.

While Mary strapped herself into the right seat and readied the charts and flight supplement, I began a thorough pre-flight inspection. I felt the invisible inspection from a pair of mother-in-law eyes in the gold Dodge at the same time.

She was a tight ship, UPX, I reassured myself as I checked the ailerons, flaps and elevators. And she ought to be. For no

52

sooner had the certification stamp dried in my logbook than the veteran 172 was delivered to Will Boles and the Brampton Flying Club Maintenance Shop. It wasn't a cheap inspection. Will's boys left no rivet unexamined, no spark plug untorqued. Over-the-shoulder seat belts were installed for the front seats, new placards were pasted on every available square inch of panel and wing and the prop was dressed and painted. The verdict?

"I expected her to be worse, frankly," Will had said, "given her age. You've got a hundred hours left to TBO, the mandatory major overhaul on that engine," he'd eyed me seriously, "and that's about what you'll get but it's still within tolerances."

It was not the kind of ringing endorsement one might hope for but if it was good enough for Will, it was good enough for me. Besides, these aircraft maintenance engineers are always cautious, I thought, as I inspected the transparent, caramel-colored oil clinging to the "full" mark on the dipstick. Ah, I mused, silently, she's a beauty, under-powered Continental engine and boat-anchor ARC radio notwithstanding. A final check of the tires and wheel pants, and in I climbed.

"Well, little family," I intoned, "this is it. The first of what I'm sure will be many adventures."

"Yeah, right, Dad," mumbled John, as he snapped, twisted and transformed Blaster from a futurist robot into a very realistic-looking cassette deck.

"Well," Mary started, hesitating a bit, "let's do it."

Brakes set. Beacon on. One shot of prime. Full rich. Throttle quarter inch. "Clear prop!" I yelled out my window, momentarily startling Johnny who thought perhaps I was beginning yet another speech. Doug Hannah had always said that most people would be mindful of spinning propellers but a good pilot always imagined a deaf-mute person had crawled under the plane just after the pilot climbed into the plane. A good, hearty yell was in order and a clear visual check as well. No human life appeared to be in danger so I turned the key, still wondering how yelling would get the attention of someone who couldn't hear.

The O-300 caught on the first revolution and rumbled to life. She sounded good. One thousand rpm. Oil pressure up. Avionics on. Controls free – "Oops, sorry Mary," I blurted, as the right hand control came back with mine and flipped the charts from her lap.

"Brampton Unicom, Uniform Papa X-Ray, radio check."

"Uniform Papa X-Ray you're five by five," the cheery female voice came back. That's strength and clarity, both five out of five. Good old radio.

"Papa X-Ray, thanks, Brampton."

The procedures Doug had drilled into me relentlessly over the past few weeks ticked through my mind in military succession. Clear front and back, I taxied to the run-up circle and swung the plane into the wind. Brakes set, rpm slowly up to seventeen hundred. Left mag check. Seventy-five rpm drop, just right. Right mag, seventy-five. Vacuum, five inches. Perfect. Lean slowly, slight increase in rpm then a sudden drop. Just like the book. Flaps full down, right, left, check. Flaps full up, right, left, check. I love this stuff! I glanced at Mary. Was she impressed? Couldn't tell. She was folding the chart into a neat square with Brampton in the dead-centre. She had a "let's get down to work" look on her face. I finished the checklist and taxied for Runway 33.

"Brampton traffic, Uniform Papa X-Ray to position 33, straight out departure." A quick visual check confirmed my passengers and gear were properly secured. Their faces registered eager anticipation — or was that well concealed concern? No matter, soon they'd share my confidence and exhilaration...okay, I'd settle for absence of terror for now. I shoved the throttle to the stops, pulled the elevator back and one hundred and forty-five horses roared into action.

Let's be fair. A 172 doesn't really *roar* into action. It sort of murmurs its way slowly up to a noisy chatter. Hmmm, this is a nice, long roll. My calculations seem to have been correct. We were indeed at gross weight. This fact was underscored by Papa X-Ray's lazy motion as her nose lifted, seemed to paused momentarily and then gently willed the rest of the aircraft into the air. Two hundred, three hundred and now four hundred feet per minute of climb. The orange rooftops of BFC slowly disappeared below and behind us.

"Brampton Unicom, Uniform Papa X-Ray is clearing your area to the north."

"Have a good trip, Papa X-Ray," a cheerful female voice radioed from below.

"Thanks, we will. See you next summer, Papa X-Ray out."

This felt good. "Here, Mary, take the controls for a bit. You own her, too." I took my hands off the yoke and smiled over at my lovely wife.

"Ahhhhh! What are you doing? Get your hands back on that thing and fly this plane!" she shrieked, half-scared and excited at the same time. I chuckled at her timidity as new pilots often do. It heightens our sense of superiority – often in the face of contradictory evidence.

Mary didn't like taking the controls at all but she liked the charts. "This is great!" she beamed. "You can see where everything is! Look, here's Collingwood on the map," she said pointing to the chart, "and there it is down there," she added pointing to "down there."

Well, at least she's happy, I thought. "And there's Meaford over there. I can see the cottage, Johnny!" she yelled over her shoulder to the back seat. "Look down there, you can see the cottage at Christie Beach!" Johnny looked up and stared momentarily at the distant lakeshore and patchwork fields, clearly unimpressed with whatever mom was going on about. "Jim, this really is...wait a minute...shouldn't Meaford be a little more east of us if we're here?" she asked, tentatively but sincerely, checking the chart against the scene below.

I winced. Let's hope this wasn't the beginning of a trend. Okay, okay, we're two hundred yards off course, give me a break, I thought, but when I opened my mouth, the "Captain" spoke.

"Well," I said, "the wind is taking us a bit off-track but we're close enough for novices."

"Why don't you just steer it back on course so we can stay on this orange line here?" she asked, innocently pointing to the track I'd laid down on the chart the night before.

Why not indeed? I shot her a look and, for a moment, saw Rick Schobesberger, Class One Instructor sitting there. "She's right, you know," he was saying. "Do you know how far two hundred yards is? Why it's..." I blinked and saw the wide-eyed innocent face of my wife waiting for an answer. "Sure, why not," I said calmly, as I corrected ten degrees west, toward Wiarton.

We didn't really have to make a fuel stop at Wiarton but full tanks always added to the security of a long flight, I was taught. The stop served to raise my passengers' confidence quotient as I executed a skillful greased landing, taxied to the ramp and over to the pumps. "Make sure you go to the bathroom," I told Johnny, firmly, "and that goes for you, too," I added, giving Mary my best pilot's look. There! Think twice about who's in charge from now on, I thought.

"Let's go, Johnny," Mary said, as she hefted our dozy son out of the passenger door. They both had taken Gravol, at my insistence. The image of Mary's pale, weakly-smiling face between retches over Pink Mountain, British Columbia on the trip down was still in my brain. Gravol tended to have a mild sedative effect on Mary, but it knocked Johnny out like a Mickey Finn. I credit Gravol for hundreds of hours of flying uninterrupted by what would have been even more, "Are we there yets?"

Up the fabulous Bruce Peninsula at 4,500 feet, a strip of Irish green dissecting the spectacular emerald waters of Georgian Bay to the east and Lake Huron to the west. Tobermory drifted past our left wing, then…the open water and the jump to Manitoulin Island. I started a climb. "Are you sure you're high enough?" Mary couldn't resist asking.

"We're at six thousand five hundred now," I responded, "any higher and we'll all get nosebleeds." It didn't take Mary long to learn that in aviation there is safety in altitude. "See that white dot down there?" I pointed a mile and a half down. "That's the ferry, for crying out loud! We could glide all the way to the Sault!"

"Really?" She looked at me and she appeared to be ready to accept my affirmation. Hmmm. This is tempting, I thought.

"No, not really," I sighed, "but we really are high enough to be safe." She shot me a look that said, "Don't trifle with me, buster! Idle talk like that will cost you points, big time!"

The weather was spectacular. Read: VFR, Ceiling And Visibility OK, or Ceiling And Visibility Unlimited. CAVOK, CAVU, any way you want to spell it, this was the kind of weather Vancouverites always said they got the day you left for home. And the wind, well, the wind was right on the nose at about twenty knots.

"When are we going to be there, Dad?"

"Not today, son."

We retraced our steps in the sky, still fresh from our trip east in June: Wawa, Thunder Bay, Kenora, Winnipeg and then – a diversion, but not to Mansfield, as I had become accustomed under Hannah's tutelage. Instead, we headed northwest across the southern tip of Lake Manitoba.

"Jim, shouldn't we be closer to the shore at this altitude?"

And on to Dauphin, Manitoba. This would be our first Lang family stop and the first in a round of fan flights that would help fill the pages in my logbook on the way home.

After brother Lin in Dauphin, we treated brother Ed and his family to rides in Yorkton, Saskatchewan. A quick "hello" and "goodbye" to Mom and Dad in Regina and it was on to Red Deer, Alberta and more friends and flights. But the school start-up date loomed and soon we were on the last leg to Fort Nelson where we planned to stay overnight, shop for groceries and set out for Nahanni the next day.

A Flight Service Specialist ruled the tower at Fort Nelson. Under his watchful eye, straight-in approaches were approved and almost the rule since little traffic clogged the airways around this northern community. I acknowledged the advisory and radioed my intentions to land on Runway 25. I had plenty of training in the procedures for approaching an uncontrolled airport and I wasn't going to screw up in front of people who knew both Papa X-Ray and me. Carefully and deliberately I over flew the field, turned around and headed back to join the mid-downwind for two-five. The Tower watched the whole process with some interest.

"Uniform Papa X-Ray, confirm you are intending to land." Was that amusement I detected in his voice?

"Affirmative," I called back, indignantly.

He might have added, "Then why don't you just quit all that flying around up there and do it?" About that moment I realized what I was doing. With an FSS, there was no need to carry out this routine. Just report on final. Blush. Oh, well, here I was on short final anyway and into a stiff breeze, too. Hey, I'll impress them with my short field landing technique, I thought. Get some respect. At the last minute I threw on full flaps, chopped the power and Papa X-Ray promptly stopped flying. Whuumph! We dropped the last two feet like a wrestler hitting the canvas. Great! The second-worst landing of my short flying career and I had to do it within sight of the very people who would see me the most often. Once again, the Blush.

"Not the best one you've done," Mary noted, evenly. Thank you very much, I thought.

We weren't yet in Nahanni Butte but already it felt like home. Ah, the north! Clean, clear air. The last bastion of freedom. Everybody knows and looks out for everybody else. Yes, sir. This was flying country and everybody knew Papa X-Ray. Airplanes are part of the fabric of everyday life and everyone knows their registrations. Only the pilots and owners changed. Over at the Esso, Hughie refueled UPX before we tied her down for the night. But not before he threw me the keys to his old Thunderbird which he regularly loaned me thereafter when I was in town.

Service was more than a mere word at this fixed base operation. No one looked after you better than these guys.

We loaded the minimal luggage needed for one night into the T-Bird and then I went inside to pay the tab. As I leaned on the counter, waiting for my bill, I scanned the local paper lying beside the till. It was the picture on the front page that had caught my eye. Hmmm. That looked like our old travel trailer in the background behind a burned-out fuel truck, I thought. "Fire Destroys Fuel Truck," the headline read. "Wait a minute," I said out loud, "that *is* our old trailer! The one I traded for the plane!"

"That's right," Hughie said, "and that's Urs' fuel truck."

"Wow! A lot's happened in the past few weeks!"

"That's not the worst," Hughie said as he took my credit card and ran it through the machine. "There was a helicopter crash up at Nahanni a few days ago. Glenn and two others were killed." Mary stepped into the office just in time to hear the last part.

"Gosh," we exclaimed, sitting down to let the news sink in.

"As far as I know," Hughie continued, "a Bell 206 crashed in poor weather while picking up Glenn and two other hunters camped on the side of a mountain. Three of the four in the chopper were pilots. Only one survived and he was badly burned and broken up."

"Who?" I asked, hoping the others were people I didn't know, but fearing the worst.

"It was Steve. I think you know him. From Fort Liard?"

"Yes, we do know him. He built the new heavy equipment shop at Nahanni. How bad is he?"

"He's burned badly but he's going to live." Hughie paused. "His girlfriend didn't make it."

Later, we drove silently into town and checked into a hotel. I'd heard of lots of aviation accidents but this was the first time I'd ever known anyone involved. It was earth-shattering news. I renewed my vow to never have anyone read about me that way as long as I could prevent it.

The next day dawned gray and drizzly. I wasn't even tempted to push this weather. It wasn't a difficult decision. We knew as never before that weather could kill. Waiting for good weather now seemed an insignificant inconvenience. Two days later, the skies cleared and we lifted off for Nahanni Butte. As we climbed for 4,500 feet we could already see the butte more than a hundred miles to the north, yellow-gold against a blue sky, reflecting the morning sun. "Are we almost there, Dad?" Johnny asked for the very last time, adding "almost" to his favourite question.

"Yes, son, we are almost there."

Fort Liard passed on the left and we thought of Glenn's widow, somewhere down there in that village. She wouldn't care much for airplanes right now or those who fly them. There had been many widows made in that part of the north and many sons who never returned to their mothers. The Nahanni River valley had claimed sightseers, outfitters and seasoned professional charter pilots. "Never turn your back on the north" the old timers would say, "and you always leave a back door open. You'll need a way out of trouble which will surely come your way sometime, if you stay long enough."

The sadness at the news of the tragedy understandably dampened our excitement at returning to Nahanni. As we descended to circuit height and passed over the settlement, it seemed to underscore the reality of living and flying in the north. This was a harsh and unforgiving land. It could bite. But as we swung to a stop in the heart of the village the laughing faces of the kids appeared, running toward the plane. Once again, our emotions were lifted by the north's other persona, its warm seductive side, its magnetic charm and magic.

"We're here!" Johnny yelled, waving at his friends who pressed against his window.

I cracked my door open, stepped out of the plane, felt the good Nahanni earth beneath my feet and slapped the mosquito already feasting on my forehead. Home at last.

# Chapter Six

# Virginia Falls

The red and white Cessna one eighty-five roared overhead toward the strip, crossed it and banked into the left-hand downwind leg for three-three. Unlike other planes that had been in and out that fall day in 1986, this one eighty-five was special. Among its passengers was our friend, Michael, the first to visit us from below 60 and, as it turned out, our only friend from the outside world who dared brave the trip to this remote part of Canada. Were one to inquire how to travel to Nahanni Butte, the plausible response would be, "You can't get there from here."

Those words might have discouraged others but they were an open challenge to globetrotting television journalists like our friend Michael. He had just returned, tanned a deep brown, from assignment in Rio de Janeiro a week or two earlier when he was sent to the Beaufort Sea to cover an oil story. Now the Beaufort Sea was more than a Sunday drive north of Nahanni Butte but to someone from central Ontario, it was practically next door. At least, that's how Michael interpreted the situation. He simply took a scheduled flight from Yellowknife to Fort Simpson and walked down to the charter operators to see if there was anything going to Nahanni. As befits his remarkable good luck, a charter bound for Nahanni Butte was already loaded with one seat to spare.

"That Lang always makes these things sound more complicated than they are," Michael must have thought as the 185 taxied up the trail into the settlement. I could see his brown face blending in well with those of his fellow passengers.

Michael always did know how to make an entrance but he outdid himself on this occasion. As the layers of passengers and luggage peeled out of the one eighty-five, he emerged last carrying a canvas bag sporting a large damp patch on the bottom.

"Lang, you old dog!" he exclaimed as we greeted via bear hug. "Good God, man, I thought the Beaufort was remote!"

"Well, you found it, didn't you? And, what's that?" I asked, pointing to the dark wet patch on his duffel bag. As I reached for it, I was hit full-face by the aroma of whiskey, sour mash whiskey, and it was coming from that bag.

"I had a little accident," he began, as I glanced from face to face. I was expecting some flicker of accusation but received neutral expressions instead. I realized I hadn't told Michael that Nahanni was a "dry" settlement. So, here's the teacher, smuggling in some booze! I needn't have worried. The people of this village seemed to hold a patent on discretion, they practised it so well. The fact that more than one of them had been in Michael's shoes at one time or another didn't hurt. "They threw the bag on the cart at Fort Simpson," he went on, "before I could tell them it was fragile and...well, I guess you can smell it, eh?"

"No problem," I replied, picking up the pace a little. "Let's just get it into the house so we can examine the damage." The Jack Daniels wasn't a total loss but to rescue it meant sucking Michael's shirts and socks dry and, since they weren't all freshly laundered, we declined. A bottle of wine survived so we set it aside for dinner, when we would do our best to get rid of the incriminating evidence. We quickly dumped the laundry into the washing machine as more pressing matters waited.

"Come on, Lang!" Michael exhorted, clapping me on the back, "Let's take that plane of yours for a ride!"

Like me, Michael was an airplane nut. I had taken him for a couple of flights out of Brampton a few weeks earlier and he was hooked, lined and sinkered. If you looked into his eyeballs, you'd have seen spinning propellers.

"Any excuse to fly," I replied. "I have a surprise for you for tomorrow but, since it's late, let's just take a hop across the river to the National Parks headquarters.

"Great! Let's go!"

"It's a really short flight," I cautioned, "but kinda neat."

"I don't care. Let's just go already! And let's take this guy, too!" Michael scooped up Johnny, threw him over his shoulder and headed for the door.

Johnny squealed with delight. "Let me down, Mike!"

Three pairs of feet crunched over the fallen leaves carpeting the path through the woods to the plane. Young Johnny ran ahead through the orange and yellow archway while Michael and I ambled behind, happily engrossed in airplane talk. His enthusiasm matched or exceeded mine and although he owned neither plane nor pilot's licence, his interest bore an uncanny resemblance to that of my earlier self.

As we stepped past the last birch into the clearing, Michael stopped, transfixed by the object of our affection, Papa X-Ray. The evening sun bathed the little 172 in a golden glow enhanced by the ring of fall colours surrounding it. Johnny, with more than fifty passenger hours under his tiny belt, trotted over to the plane. I unlocked the door and he scrambled in, settled in his seat and placed his ever-present Transformer within easy reach. A first time visitor, Michael could appreciate the idyllic setting, which Johnny, like most of the residents of Nahanni Butte, tended to take for granted.

Michael eagerly followed me through my pre-flight inspection with reporter-like questions about airfoils and engines.

"Do you have to gas up?"

"Nope. Up here, I make a point of topping off the tanks every time I complete a trip, no matter how short. That way the fuel stays free of moisture and you're always ready to go."

"These your fuel drums here?" he asked, kicking the drums at the side of the clearing.

"Yeah, I bought them from Greg the outfitter," I replied, as I herded Michael over to the plane. "He runs his operation for a few months each year, taking hunters north to try for sheep and caribou." We settled into the plane, and strapped in.

"So, there's another guy here with a plane?"

"For the summer, yeah. He has a Maule on floats and a pretty yellow Super Cub that he's taken up river today to supply his guests in their hunting camp. Guys like you, Mike!"

"I'm no hunter!" he balked at the very idea. "I'd never murder a moose!"

Ah, city-folk, I thought. I teased him at bit. "Well, we've tried eating them without shooting them first and they put up one heck of a fight!" We laughed.

We taxied out onto the strip trailing a shower of yellow leaves to backtrack the short distance for Runway 13. I swung Papa X-Ray around, checked that everyone was strapped in and eased on the power.

"Yahoo!" shouted Michael, "Let's go!" He noticed I was adding power very slowly and commented, "That's not how you did it in Brampton!"

I brought the power up to full after a few more seconds and yelled, "You have to keep your nose up and add power gradually on these gravel strips or you'll pay for it with a dented prop!"

"Yahoo!" he shouted again.

Johnny chimed in, "Yahoo!"

As we blasted skyward, I pointed out another major difference between flying here and most places in Canada.

"Look down," I instructed. "If we lose power now, we've got nothing but bush and water below us. Once you're airborne up here," I pointed out, "there are precious few choices for forced landings."

He nodded agreement as he surveyed the carpet of primeval forest. Climbing out in a lazy arc, I leveled off at one thousand AGL and pointed UPX toward the sheer rock face of the Butte just a few hundred yards away.

A minute later, we were over the cluster of red log buildings nestled between the river's edge and the base of the Butte on a left-hand downwind for the 1900-foot packed sand airstrip.

"You said it was a short flight," Michael shouted over the engine, "but this is ridiculous!"

I laughed as I dropped the nose and aimed for the residences to do a noisy downwind low and over.

"Hey, are you sure you know what you're doing here, Lang?"

"Not to worry," I laughed again. "I want to let the folks know I'm here. See," I continued, pointing to the runway, "the strip borders the buildings and the wardens often use it as a road. Their kids use it as a playground." I pulled up and angled right to allow enough room for a decent approach.

"Nice setup those guys have down there," Michael commented, "and they get, like a handful of visitors every year."

"Well, you know how expensive it is to get here," I answered. "Not everyone works for the CBC."

Michael coughed in mock indignation.

We climbed out over the river. I began a wide left-hand downwind for a westward landing. Michael took in the scenery and experience in silence while Johnny, playing quietly in the back seat, was oblivious to the panorama below. Lining up on final wasn't a straightforward procedure. In fact, using this strip was tricky for a pilot of my double-digit flying time but you learned quickly in the north and I had practised this before. I stabilized my approach at seventy miles per hour and a five-hundred-foot-per-minute descent rate. I lined up with a building to the left of where the runway numbers would have been, if there had been runway numbers.

"I'm too young to die!" Michael cried out, half-serious, shielding his face with his hands.

"Say your prayers, buddy," I laughed, as I set up for the unconventional approach created by a large stand of trees which effectively blocked the path on short final. A convenient notch had been cut out on the left side of the bush allowing the skillful aviator to slip through. Michael gripped the handhold above his door as I side-slipped, power off. The slipstream whistled through the doors. We cleared the gap. I stabbed left rudder for a right-hand slip, then down into the flare for a landing as pretty as the scenery.

"I'm impressed!" Michael gasped as we rolled to a stop near the park office.

"All in a day's work up here," I replied, matter-of-factly.

"Yeah, right, Lang!" Michael shot back, but he was showing more respect than usual.

Johnny stayed in the back seat while Michael and I climbed out and took in the surroundings. "Isn't this the place Dick Turner built?" he asked. We didn't notice the tall, uniformed man who had ambled up behind us.

"This was the original homestead of Dick Turner," replied Doug, the Park Warden. Michael spun around to see who was answering his question. I introduced him to Doug, a frequent visitor to the settlement side and an all around good guy.

"I didn't realize you knew about Dick," I said to Michael.

"You told me about him, Lang," Michael responded, sarcastically. "He used to trap up here and he wrote a book about his adventures flying around up here, right?"

"That's right," Doug said, as we sauntered over to his office building. It was a one-storey log structure, every inch the image of a parks office. "He built this strip for his own plane and he used to operate a store right on this spot."

Michael wandered about while Doug and I exchanged bits of news and gossip. The sun had already disappeared around the northwest corner of the Butte. It was time to go.

You don't hope for a successful departure from the parkside strip. You have to know precisely the position and location of wheels, trees and river at lift-off for there is precious little room for error. Michael was in his glory as I recited the short-field departure technique.

Papa X-Ray parked beside the school master's house in Nahanni Butte, Northwest Territories. The Lang's three-year-old son Johnny is playing in foreground.

Mary and Johnny Lang settle aboard the Islander that took them on their first flight to Nahanni Butte.

Nahanni Butte, NWT, population 75, on the Nahanni River.

The Lang & Ackroyd Band circa 1979. Jim and Mary Lang are second from the right.

The view from the Lang's front yard, the Nahanni River and the Nahanni "Butte".

This is the Charles Yohin School, the new two-room school that Lang moved into with his students during his first year.

"Flaps 20 degrees. Stand on the brakes with the tail in the weeds and apply full power," I intoned, "then release brakes and pray!"

We lurched forward toward the stand of pines that marked the western boundary. The airspeed needle touched 60 at the last building and I hauled Papa X-Ray off. I kept one eye on the airspeed and tach, noting the little Continental O-300 was successfully pulling the tach needle through 2400 rpm.

"Yahoo!" Michael yelled, as our wheels cleared the tallest pine by more than fifty feet. "It might be a short flight but it's a good 'un!" he shouted above the straining engine. I banked right, over the river and into the downwind for three-three.

Later, as we put Papa X-Ray to bed, I pulled out my log book. "You're going to log that trip?" Michael asked, surprised.

"Point three hours," I replied jotting the time, number of passengers, weight and signature in the book.

"And a damn fine point three it was, too!" Michael pronounced. Johnny was already trundling on up the path back to the village. Later we eliminated the evidence as we discussed my surprise adventure, planned for tomorrow.

"Virginia Falls?" Michael was delighted. "Wow! This will be great! I've never seen it, have you?"

"Not yet," I replied. In fact, some people lived their entire lives on the banks of the Nahanni River and died never having been there. Tourists paid a king's ransom to trek by canoe, boat or plane, one hundred and eighty winding miles north to where the mighty cataract performed twenty-four hours a day to an empty house.

After a year in Nahanni Butte we were eager to see the Falls at last and now we had no excuses. Michael certainly was game, aided by blissful ignorance of what the trip entailed. Mary, on the other hand, knew precisely what we had bitten off. As we climbed to sixty-five hundred feet the next morning, she did little to hide her apprehension.

"Higher, Jim," she instructed, eyeing the inhospitable mountains below us.

"Yes, dear." I was grateful to be going at all so I didn't mind sacrificing a little altitude for a lot of wifely good will.

"How far is it?" Michael asked, snapping pictures from the right seat.

"Three hundred and twenty miles round trip," I answered, tactfully avoiding mentioning that for the full length of the trip there would be nothing but hostile mountains, trees and the Nahanni River to soften a forced landing. Well, almost nothing. There was the Cadillac strip but I was saving that surprise for later.

Mary, who loved the experience over all but who remained dutifully concerned about safety, was somewhat appeased by the day – a glorious clear blue wonder with not a breath of wind to ruffle UPX's feathers. On windy days these mountains could produce howling winds and turbulence that could toss an aircraft like a paper cup. But not today. Today was perfect.

Four eager faces peered through the Plexiglas at the panorama of river and mountains parading silently below us. In a moment of weakness I pleaded for a lower altitude but my wife was immovable on the subject. After all, she'd agreed to come along with Michael and me on this brilliant Saturday morning. She'd even agreed to bring our only child, delicate flesh and blood. She demanded but one condition — altitude.

"Yes, dear."

We wound through the valley above the great canyons made famous by the adventures of Albert Faille in his quest for gold. We floated over vistas rarely seen except as filmed by the National Film Board. These scenes had been enjoyed by the moneyed elite, including Pierre Trudeau and HRH Prince Edward, who had paddled the fabled river below in more recent times. Did the mountains under our wheels hide secret gold deposits? None had been found in spite of decades of prospecting and persistent rumors made more persistent by authors such as Pierre Berton. Locals still chuckled at his now-famous description of "Headless Valley," a name he purportedly coined on the spot when his pilot set down on a sandbar in Deadman's Valley.

Pictures of crumpled airplanes and broken bodies formed and re-formed in my mind, as I silently recalled Dick Turner's descriptions of the many wrecks that punctuated the Nahanni River Valley. Hidden from view, they were mute testimony to the poor judgment of pilots who came before me and never returned. I checked the altimeter.

"What's that, a cloud?" Michael asked, using his telephoto lens as a telescope. Dead ahead, an unusual stationary cloud rose in the otherwise clear blue sky. Suddenly I knew what it was.

"That's not a cloud," I shouted, my heart leaping, "it's mist, mist from the Falls!"

66

Glancing furtively at Mary, who was straining to get a better look, I carefully set up for a descent — down to 1000 feet above ground. This would be low enough to appreciate the perspective and majesty of the highest waterfall in Canada without risking life and limb at the hands of my determined spouse.

We cleared the canyon wall and...there it was! Virginia Falls!

"What an awesome sight!" Michael exclaimed, snapping more and more pictures. Awesome indeed. Almost twice the height of Niagara, it thundered silently below our wings. We flew over the Falls and started a slow turn to follow the cascading water back down. Above the falls, the Nahanni, swollen with run-off from its headwaters hundreds of miles to the north and wild with white-water rapids, raced toward the precipice, where it plunged headlong into a massive conical rock. A hundred feet high and three hundred wide, this immovable block of granite perched at the very lip of the drop where it split the water in two, leaving it to plunge three hundred feet to the river below. Few had witnessed this natural wonder and now four more names were added to that short list.

I circled carefully as my passengers continued to take pictures – all except Johnny who wondered in his three-year-old fashion what the fuss was all about. Then it was time to turn around and head back – but not home, not just yet. I had planned a surprise stop at the Cadillac Mine on Prairie Creek about halfway back to the Butte. It wouldn't be hard to find. Greg Williams had provided clear directions. After a glance at Mary, who seemed to be warming to the adventure, we turned left at "the gate" and headed over the rounded mountaintops to the Cadillac strip.

"So this is why you packed a big lunch and the fishing rods," she said accusingly. "You're pretty sneaky, Jim Lang!"

"Why would there be a strip in such a godforsaken place as this?" Michael asked, mystified but eager for more adventure.

"There's an abandoned mine down there and they used the strip to supply the operation," I answered. But where was this strip, I wondered, as I stared down into the dark, narrow valley ahead and below?

"There it is!" Michael answered my silent question and pointed down; way, way down to a gray line on the valley floor, four thousand feet below. This is going to be interesting, I thought, as I brought the power back and slid the plane down into the wedge between the rising valley walls.

Ears popping, I leveled out at a thousand feet and overflew the 3,000 foot gravel runway, flanked on one side by a gentle creek and on the other by the sharply rising mountainside. Similar to the strip at Parkside, this one offered a dipsy-doodle on approach, which I was planning to make from the opposite end. But just getting lined up presented a challenge. The narrow valley afforded little room to turn around so, with the strip behind us, I climbed for altitude before turning and setting up a long, steep descent toward the rock outcrop that marked the near end of the runway. A quick sideslip and flare and the dark shadows of the valley closed around us as the wheels touched on the rough gravel surface and we rolled to a gentle stop.

Mags off, electrics off, I looked up and studied the scene for a moment while my passengers jumped from the plane and started to explore the place. I stepped out and scanned the departure paths off both ends of the runway. Would I have attempted such a landing had I seen it from this perspective first? I wondered, looking up at the peaks to the right and left. I grew even more dubious as I scanned down the valley, our ultimate take-off path, to where the blue sky appeared high in a small "v" far ahead. My passengers no doubt assumed it would be a piece of cake as the first part of the day had been. I rested on Greg's assurances and joined Mary, Michael and Johnny as they picked their way over the boulders and down to the creek to tempt the trout rumoured to lurk in these burbling waters.

The rumours should be well founded. This Cadillac strip was, after all, well touched by human hands. The Cadillac mining company had tried in vain to coax ore-bearing rock from these valley walls and evidence of their passing was in abundant supply. Shacks, oil drums and assorted machinery decorated the south side of the strip which, in its day, had received Douglas DC-3s laden with men and machinery. DC-3s! My mind reeled as I pictured the lumbering twin-engine airplanes duplicating our landing. My one-hundred-hour total flying time was beginning to have an effect on my confidence and not a positive one.

"Here, fishy, fishy!" Johnny sang, tugging on his fishing line. "Dad, where are the fish?" he asked, implying that I could somehow do something about the absence of bites. But, the fish – were they there at all – would not be fooled on this occasion so we made do with a "fisherman's lunch" brought in as a hedge against that very possibility. In spite of rumours of trout, like most people of the village, I was a skeptic. Prairie Creek ran into the Nahanni and for all its magnificence, its silty water was devoid of all fish except the lowly "losh," a dogfish-like creature. Although tasty, the losh could never be confused with a sport-fish. The general absence of fish underscored the harsh reality behind the beauty of the region. As oldtimers would say, remembering starvation and hardship, "You can't eat the scenery."

But you can eat lunch. As soon as the last morsel disappeared down young Johnny's throat we made our way back to UPX, my mind not a little absorbed with the takeoff to come. Greg-the-outfitter had told me about this great valley and suggested I take Prairie Canyon on my way out. "It leaves a good hundred feet or so between the canyon walls and the wingtips," he had said, "and it's quite a sight. Just make sure there's no turbulence."

Yeah, right. Greg routinely landed his Super Cub in alpine meadows and on sandbars in the middle of the river. No doubt to him this would be a walk in the park. Some walk. Some park.

"Okay, everybody strapped in?" I called out to my three passengers, jostling themselves into their nests amid fishing poles and camera bags.

"What's 'density altitude'?" Michael asked. Oops. Guess I was thinking out loud again.

"Uh, well, it's a function of heat, altitude and...uh, let's put it this way. It takes a longer roll to get airborne the higher the strip's elevation and the warmer the day."

"And we're pretty high here, eh?"

"Yeah, pretty high." I answered. Better think this through carefully.

"But, we're at half fuel so our weight is good. And it's a relatively cool day and that's good, too." But the altimeter showed that sea level was well below us and that wasn't good. But it was good enough.

"Yahoo!" Michael called out, in his now trademark cry, as I firewalled the engine. Gravel flew in our wake and as we roared down the strip, I could see there wouldn't be a great deal of spare air between our wheels, traveling at 70 mph, and the stationary trees below.

"Whew! Pretty close, eh?" Michael commented.

"Well, not really," I told a half-truth. We were climbing steadily if not quickly and I knew that the river flowed down from here and that, no matter what, we would make it all right. Nevertheless, as the altimeter showed an anemic four-hundred-feet-per-minute climb rate, the shallow "v" ahead allowed an unnervingly tight departure path. I banked around the rising terrain and as the familiar rounded top of the mountain that had greeted our arrival loomed ahead, I decided to go back the way we had come.

"I thought you said you were going to take Prairie Creek Canyon," Mary shouted from the back seat.

Now, that's interesting, I thought. Of all people to ask such a question. I guess she couldn't see what I was seeing up front, or she wouldn't have asked.

"Naw, I'd rather just take the route I know for sure," I tossed back, thinking, Prairie Creek Canyon must be interesting indeed if it is more breathtaking than this. And just too darned interesting for this cub aviator!

The remainder of the trip was anti-climactic. Not many flights could equal the Falls and Cadillac experiences. Four beaming faces emerged from Papa X-Ray that late afternoon. Among them, one was sporting a new look, the look of the aviation-smitten. Michael was thoroughly hooked.

In the slow-motion rhythm of the north, his visit seemed over before it had started. But it was long enough to plant the flying bug firmly in Michael's belly. To make sure he'd been properly bitten, I offered to fly him to Fort Nelson the next morning. In fact, I offered to let him do most of the flying.

The glorious fall weather obliged, delivering another picture postcard of the north as we lifted off Runway 15 for the familiar one-hundred-and-fifty-mile flight. "It's like sailing a boat, isn't it?" he cooed, as he tried his hand at tracking the course in a slight crosswind.

I didn't answer. I just smiled. Yup. He'd been bitten, and good.

I explained every move and procedure as I lined up for Runway 07 at Fort Nelson. Michael absorbed every word. The flying bug was worming its way deep in his psyche in spite of my warning that it was a trap. I alluded to "holes to throw money into" and the vagaries of weather. I warned him, not too sternly, that he was destined to fall victim to aviationitis, just as I had.

As he waited for his connecting flight back to civilization, I looked down to see him standing by the Esso dealer, eyes shielded against the sun, watching me climb out on my way back to Nahanni. Neither of us knew then that an aircraft figured in his future. But, knowing Michael, he wouldn't let a passion for new adventure pass him by.

70

In hindsight, it was unfair in the extreme to introduce him to flying the way I had. Why, there'd be an airplane in every garage in the country if everyone had the chance to visit Virginia Falls as we had. I dialed CBC radio on the ADF and pointed Papa X-Ray's nose toward the Butte.

# Chapter Seven

# Grocery run

"And don't forget to finish your math for homework!" my voice echoed through the emptying school as the last of my twenty-two students disappeared out the door. It was Friday afternoon and we were just into our second winter in Nahanni Butte.

"We won't! Have a good weekend, Mr. Lang!" came the cheery response. We won't, indeed, the teacher in me repeated to myself, skeptically. I hope Mary has that snowmobile running, I thought, as I did a quick round of my little schoolhouse.

An award-winning architect designed the building, Duffy contracted the construction and I supervised the move into it. Charles Yohin School, named after a revered, deceased Nahanni elder, was a complicated modern log structure but it employed simple, efficient use of space. By dividing the square log building diagonally the architect had created two triangular classrooms. Huge logs formed the corner roof beams and natural pine finished the interior walls. The skylights represented the only serious design flaw. As welcome as natural light was, in order to show a film or slides, teachers needed to be able to make a room dark. On most school days in the north, and particularly in the spring with twenty-four hour daylight, skylights rendered that impossible. And when it rained, they leaked. I learned to curse those skylights.

To create a dark viewing space, we arranged the large wheeled clothes closets that did double-duty as chalk-boards and parked them under the second floor balcony. There we'd huddle, almost cozy, as I conducted lessons using slides, film, video or filmstrips. Such close proximity led to no small amount of rib-poking, sniggering and the resulting remedial action of the teacher but the kids obviously loved the break from routine.

My second-floor office loft straddled the two rooms. On the primary side, Grades One through Three, a Plexiglas wall separated me from the action below. A steel cable railing offered Grades Four through Eight no such insulation on the other side.

This proved particularly handy for me as, with the able help of Laura, my classroom assistant, I taught both rooms simultaneously and served as principal, too. When the growing pile of brown envelopes and papers on my desk beckoned, I could work upstairs and supervise both rooms from my lofty perch. "Let's have a little work, shall we, Wesley?" my voice would boom down from on high, as the little pupil spun around, trying to locate the source of the edict.

From time to time Johnny would wander over to the school and I'd settle him in upstairs where he'd play and often watch dad in action with the older grades. Occasionally, I'd stop in the middle of a lesson, when I'd see the Grade Eight students pointing over my head and laughing out loud. I'd spin around in time to see Johnny leaning on the cables and making faces at me behind my back. Not yet four years old and already a critic.

Today, I had to hurry. Furnace set, water turned off, out the door I burst and was caught full in the face by the rope hanging loosely from the old CPR train bell I had positioned above the front door. As I secured the rope I noted the flag hanging limply from the pine pole the students and I had stripped and planted beside the main entrance. The flag flew twenty-four hours a day but not only out of national pride. The airstrip lacked a windsock and when the Chinooks blew out of the west, the school flag would confirm the inevitable crosswind to inbound pilots passing low over the village.

I took the stairs by threes and headed for the house when I saw Mary on the Ski-Doo, roaring out of our yard, and turned to head her off. The machine lurched forward, engine roaring and then stopped abruptly. It was clear she did not yet have the hang of the thumb-throttle.

"How do you control this thing?" she shouted above the noisy beast, as I slipped in front of her onto the seat. Johnny, bundled into his winter cocoon, sat nonchalantly in the sled, now twisted sideways from the erratic ride. I gently squeezed the throttle and we were off to the strip.

"You just have to squeeze it gently," I said.

"It never works for me," she returned loudly, and that was it.

I had closed the school a little early to allow us time to get to Fort Nelson before dark but it would still be tight. The sun was already heading toward the mountainous western horizon when we roared up to UPX nestled in its snowy clearing beside the strip. Although it was relatively warm, only minus fifteen or so, my

73

portable generator and car preheater warmed the engine from noon
to the last recess. I used the recess time to collect the generator,
slip off the army-surplus parachute wing covers, run to the house,
fire up the radiophone and file my flight plan. Every minute
counted on Friday afternoon flights!

"Okay, Mary, climb in and let's get out of here!" I commanded, as I popped the doors and tossed Johnny into the back
seat. I whipped the orange cowl-cover off and stuffed it in the rear
cargo bay, jumped in and slammed the door. I glanced at the crew.
"Everybody strapped in?" Nods all around. One revolution and the
still-warm Continental fired, shattering the afternoon silence and
blasting snow into the bush behind us.

"Next time, let's just go on Saturday," Mary commented, as
we taxied for one-five. "This rushing around is crazy!" She adjusted her new Telex headset and was testing the intercom with her
observations and advice.

I'd bought myself a new David Clark headset and Telexes for
the crew. No more shouting over the cabin noise. No more, "Say
agains!" to controllers. No more, "Sorry, dear, can't hear you!"
Now there was no escaping the running commentary.

"But we lose the whole weekend that way," I objected,
cranking Papa X-Ray around and lining her up with the runway.
"We can't get down, buy the groceries and get back before dark in
one day." I squeezed on the power. "Okay, here we go!"

UPX climbed out through the thick, cold air with authority.
Rising into the azure, late afternoon sky, our frantic pace and tension evaporated as we took in the beauty of the northern winter
scene. Even Johnny seemed enthralled and as he struggled to
adjust his new headset, I expected adjectives of wonder to fill the
new intercom.

"Are we there yet, Dad?" the little voice piped up in the
centre of my head.

"No, son, not yet. Why don't…" I started to suggest, when
strange gurgling, humming and sucking sounds filled my headset.
Hmmm, it seems he likes the intercom, I thought.

"Sunny Day, chasing the…clouds away!" he sang, and soon
we were all singing the Sesame Street song.

"Can you tell me how to get, how to get to…?"

"Are you sure we can make Fort Nelson before dark?" Mary
interrupted, as she flipped open the chart and began to check refer-
ences with the ground below.

"Mom! Don't interrupt!" came the command from the back.

"How to get to Sesame Streeeeeet!"

Always cautious, Mary was comforted by the unmistakable lights of Fort Nelson, visible from more than thirty miles in the fading light. I dialed 122.2 on the ARC.

"Fort Nelson Radio, Uniform Papa X-Ray, over." There was a short pause, then a clear, loud voice filled my headset.

"Fort Nelson Radio, Uniform Papa X-Ray, go ahead." Wow! These headsets are great! I thought.

"Fort Nelson, Papa X-Ray now approximately twenty-five miles north, landing Fort Nelson, over."

"Papa X-Ray, Fort Nelson, altimeter three zero zero five, winds favouring two-five, report intended runway, over."

"We'll take two-five."

"Roger that, Papa X-Ray, call final for two-five."

I smiled at the simplicity of landing at an airport supervised by a Flight Service Specialist. It had most of the benefits of a control zone and all of the benefits of not having a control zone. Of course, the FSS also would notice that only a vivid imagination could describe the sun as being above the horizon at this point. For my part, I'd describe it as daylight on a cloudy day, perhaps. He could question my credentials, of course. I held no night endorsement, and he likely knew it, as pretty much everybody at this airport knew about the "crazy teacher who traded his trailer for that old 172 , you remember, Papa X-Ray?"

Oh, well, I thought, next summer I'll get that night endorsement and put all this iffy stuff to rest. Then I dropped full flaps on short final and used the thick cold air to cushion the touchdown, rolling just past the numbers before executing a sharp right hand turn for Taxiway Bravo.

"You're getting good at those landings, Sweetie." Mary smiled. She leaned over and gave me a little peck on the cheek.

"Thank you, dear." I accepted her compliment, then closed my flight plan and taxied to the Esso dealer where we would refuel and tie-down for the night. Our trusty Esso agent heard our radio call from twenty miles out and actually made a point of staying late to take care of us. Always a most thoughtful operator, he dropped us at our hotel before heading home himself. They threw away the mold when they made that fine gentleman.

Next stop – dinner! "Hamaburger," Johnny said. He always ordered "hamaburger" in restaurants and had no intention of making an exception in the hotel restaurant that evening.

"You won't be able to eat anything if you keep drinking the creamers," I said, as he peeled the top off his third little plastic cup and downed the white stuff.

"I think I'm going to be sick," Mary groaned jokingly while surreptitiously slipping a couple of foil-packed ketchups into her purse. "Well, they're real handy on the road," she said defensively, catching my feigned look of disapproval. Do other people plan for emergencies like this woman? I asked myself. Not one, but three packs of candles filled our glove compartment in the truck, parked at Fort Simpson. And we had enough flares in the emergency kit in the plane to mark our name, address and postal code in the snow, should we ever be down in the bush, God forbid, some day.

"Eat your hamaburger, I mean hamburger," she said to Johnny, as he reached for the last of the creamers. Ah, the country cousins in the big city. I did a quick visual check around the crowded room. Nope, nobody seemed to notice anything unusual. A more detailed check showed why. Everybody was a little strange. This was Fort Nelson, hub of the north, where New Yorkers, en route to Alaska, rubbed shoulders with trappers blinking in the harsh glare of civilization after months in the bush. The man in the tattered snowmobile suit, his wife swaddled in sweaters and scarves and the little kid drinking coffee creamers fit right in.

"I know we've got more time than usual," my wife, the organizer, announced in the lobby the next morning, "but we have a lot to do." I took that as "I intend to Christmas shop!" and counted my blessings for having an excuse to avoid that accursed job. I determined early in our marriage that women were born with a "shopping gene". Their only culpability in the trait remained their tireless efforts to involve men in this insufferable activity. Men, of course, were born with the much more useful, "aviation gene." At least, the good ones were.

"I'll get the groceries," I volunteered, maybe a bit too cheerfully, "and meet everyone back here in the lobby. The hotel-owner said he'd be happy to drive us back to the airport around noon."

"Noon? Why so early?" Mary asked.

"Because," I explained, "we're in a different time zone and noon here is one o'clock in Nahanni and it takes more than an hour and a half to get there and it gets dark just after..."

"Okay, okay, I get it! Noon, then. Geez, we'd better get at it," she said, taking Johnny's hand. "Come on, Johnny," and the two colourful figures trundled off down the street. "No, you can't have another Transformer," I heard her admonish as I headed for the Overwaitea. Next time I'd shop the IGA. I tried to spread the money around. Two grocery stores were better than one and competition kept the prices down. It was Overwaitea's turn this time.

The check-out cashier and the manager noticed me as soon as I ambled through the door. Their looks revealed both delight and trepidation. They knew me here, all right. I had arrived many times with a thousand dollars and only an hour to spend it, and the resulting confusion had people scurrying for cases of milk and eggs while I frantically tried to adhere to Mary's shopping list.

"Not to worry," I said to the manager as he approached, warily, "I've actually got more than two hours today!"

"Glad to hear it," he replied, "but if we can help, don't hesitate to ask."

"Thanks, but I'll be okay," I said, as I grabbed my first shopping cart.

One by one, I added to the line of bulging shopping carts that snaked up to the last cashier at the end row. Three more aisles to go, I said to myself, fingering the shopping list. I had long since learned to not follow the list. Following the list meant running first to one end of the store for vanilla and then to the other for cabbage. Not only was this inefficient, it meant these items would end up in the same cart. No, no, no! That's not how it's done at all. One aisle at a time, that's how it's done. One cart is for canned goods, another for produce, another for meat and so on.

Most people were concerned that they were getting less and less for their grocery dollar. They stood at the till, alternately staring in amazement at their small piles of groceries and at the smaller stack of change in their hands. Not me. The smaller the pile of groceries, the better. This all would have to fit in the plane, after all.

"Just six carts this time," I announced to the startled cashier who had just begun her shift. She obviously knew nothing of this weird northerner and his shopping habits.

"I'll take him, Joyce," said Pearl, my usual cashier, as she slipped into position behind the till. "This takes some getting used to. Bags, not boxes, right?" she asked, as the manager showed up to take the bag-boy's job. I guess I'd already told her that it was a lot easier to tuck bags than boxes into the nooks and crannies of old UPX.

"Not quite as many as usual," he noted.

"Got the wife and kid this time, not as much room for useful cargo," I chuckled. "Let's get started, Pearl."

As I wheeled the first cart of bags over near the door, the assembly line was in full swing. Mercifully the manager steered unwary shoppers away from Pearl. She was a check-out dervish. The fingers on her right hand flew over the keys while her left hand flung the bacon, beans and celery to the manager. He really knew how to pack a good bag. Never got the eggs on the bottom or the canned food on top of the bread. Must be why he was the manager.

"Nine hundred and sixty-two dollars and forty cents," I estimated as Pearl's finger hovered over the "total" key.

"Too much," she ventured, fixing me with an impish grin.

"I agree," said the manager. We played the little game I'd started on my first visit. I always tried to guess the total, just for the fun of it. One time I got it to within ten cents and won, well, nothing. But I won.

The finger dropped and the machine chinged.

"Nine zero five fifty-five! You're way off this time, Laddie," Pearl laughed as I wrote out the check.

"Got all six carts?" I asked, a little suspiciously.

"Hey, you lost. Take it like a man," she leveled at me.

I hefted the last bag onto the sidewalk outside the Overwaitea when Mary rolled up in the hotel manager's car. A half hour later we were unloading our booty beside the plane. Hmm, there is a lot of stuff, here. Shopping! Oh well, it would be tight, but doable, I thought.

"Are we going to get it all in?" Mary asked, sizing up the pile of groceries and then her own pile of Christmas shopping.

"No sweat," I answered, "and if we do drop out of the sky from the sheer weight of it, just think of how long we could live in the bush with all this stuff." I was kidding, of course, but one should not kid with one's wife about these things.

"Jim," she cautioned.

"Don't worry," I laughed, "if it's too much we'll just leave the kid behind. He's almost four and should start thinking about getting a job and getting out on his own."

"Da-aad! Let me in that plane!" Johnny scrambled up the gear leg and crawled into his car-seat/plane-seat.

I eyed Papa X-Ray. Okay, maybe it was a bit heavy, but still under gross, probably. I mean, who actually weighs groceries? Bad question.

"Here's the scale," Mary said, producing our bathroom scale from one of her many cloth bags. Yes, she actually brought the scale along and, because my weight, at 200 pounds, was the easiest to subtract from the total, I was compelled to stand dutifully on the scale and hold the groceries while Mary totaled the score.

I looked left and right. My mind wandered. Please, let no one see me doing this. Well, maybe let Transport Canada see me but they'd probably object to the scale.

I mentally pictured a man in the gray suit approaching us. We're from Transport Canada and we're here to help. I vaguely heard Mary say, "Good, now the next bag."

Weighing in, are we? I imagined the government official would ask. Of course, you realize that you need to certify that bathroom scale which is clearly marked 'not for commercial use'. Nice try, I thought.

This is not a commercially-licensed aircraft, I pounced on the hallucination, and besides, I'm not commercially licensed either, so there! And another thing, while you're here...

"Jim, that's it and here's the total," Mary's voice broke the trance.

"Oh, thank you, dear, let's see, yes, it looks fine," I replied. Actually, it was good to know just exactly how heavy the load was. And secretly I was grateful for her thoroughness and for her company. But if I didn't give her a hard time about it she might think she'd awakened in the wrong bed.

Johnny's feet rested on two bags of meat while the mound of remaining groceries, tied down with ropes and bungee cords, touched the headliner beside him as we taxied onto two-five.

But, what was this? "Fort Nelson Radio, Uniform Papa X-Ray, come in."

"Fort Nelson, go ahead, Papa X-Ray."

"Roger, Fort Nelson, confirm there is a wolf on the numbers here at Runway two-five, over." There was a long pause as we gazed at the big timber wolf standing proudly on the big white "2". He returned our look just as intently, with no indication that he was prepared to clear a path for us.

"Uniform...Papa...X-Ray," the slow, hesitant voice came back, "it would appear that you might get a nice fur coat out of the deal if you elected to add power at this point...nice size and colour."

"Johnny, look, a wolf!" Mary shouted excitedly.

"Yeah, a wolf!" Johnny shouted in response, his eyes wide.

79

"What are you going to do, Jim?"

I throttled up to make some noise. The wolf would not budge. It was a stand-off. UPX was pointed down two-five and the wolf, fifty feet ahead, was pointed directly at UPX.

"Uniform Papa X-Ray, rolling on two-five," I radioed, "perhaps he can be motivated to give way."

"Jim! Are you sure...?" Mary started, then thought better of getting involved here.

"Wolves are very intelligent creatures, I've always been told," I reasoned, "and no intelligent creature is going to deliberately get involved with a big metal beast making as much noise as us!" I added power. The wolf turned and began to lope and then to run down the runway but only at the last second did he veer out of our path.

"Missed him," the Flight Service Specialist came back. "Have a good trip, Papa X-Ray."

The thick, cold air and western breeze easily offset the effects of the "shopping gene" as we lifted off halfway down the runway, climbed to the west and then banked north. Ah, the excitement of flying the bush. My eyes lazily roamed over the rivers and streams that passed below us as we settled down to cruise at forty-five hundred feet in the still afternoon air.

"Isn't this...fun...?" my voice trailed off as I caught a glimpse of my sleeping navigator. A quick glance revealed that our young son had joined her in dreamland. No navigator. How *would* I find my way home? Easy now, don't be too cute, she can read minds — probably even while she sleeps.

"Wake up! We're almost home!" I announced over the intercom, as I lined up on final for the Butte an hour later. The bodies stirred, eyes blinked in the fading light on the brilliant snow.

"Are we...?"

"Yes, son, we are there yet," I answered, my good humour still intact after an unexpectedly quiet flight.

Hmmm, that full-flap landing was so nice yesterday. I should try it again, I mused. In fact, every landing should be a full-flap landing, right? Right, I thought as I dropped the full forty degrees. I'd kiss this baby on so sweetly they'll only know they're down when the prop stops. I had done a quick circuit to check the runway and, although it had snowed overnight, it didn't look deep enough to worry about. I reveled in my advanced technique, expecting nothing unusual when the wheels touched.

But, what's this? It feels like we're in ten inches of snow! "The snow is too deep!" I exclaimed to no one in particular, hammering on the power to hold the nose up. I felt the plane dragging as if someone had just tossed out an anchor. At the last second, it started to veer sharply left. My crew, just barely awake, was uncharacteristically and blessedly silent. I chopped the power and the plane stopped dead. I cracked the door and stepped out, expecting deep new snow. Instead, I looked down to see barely a scant inch of the fluff under my mukluks.

Then I noticed the skid mark. My left wheel had not rotated one inch since touchdown. A long skid-mark described my unexpected short-field landing, perhaps one hundred feet in total. I knelt down and examined the left wheel. Sure enough, it was a frozen brake that nearly wrecked our day, not deep snow. I couldn't have chosen a worse time to try my gentle short-field technique. Had I landed with a solid thump, the way I usually did, the brake would have broken free on impact. But, no, I had to try to grease it on and the resulting kid-glove treatment had almost put us in the ditch.

"Can I help?" Mary asked, sounding more composed than I would have expected under the circumstances.

"I can handle it," I grumped and gave the wheel a kick. The brake came free immediately and I climbed back into the plane for the short taxi into our parking spot.

"Did you try a different kind of landing or something?" she asked innocently.

"Why don't you go get the Ski-Doo," I suggested, changing the subject, "and just squeeze that throttle gently, okay?"

# Chapter Eight

# Father Mary

Father Mary is an unusual name. It might help to remember that Catholic nuns often take gender-opposite names such as Sister George, or Sister Mary Herman. In Father Mary's case, however, he was born with the surname, Mary.

Father Pierre Mary of Paris, ("a little town you may 'ave 'eard of in France," as he would tell new acquaintances), arrived in the Nahanni-Fort Liard area of the Northwest Territories in the early nineteen fifties. On a mission from his Father Superior of the Oblates of Mary Immaculate, he was to represent the Catholic Church and attend to the spiritual needs of the faithful in this remote land, many thousands of miles west and north of his native France. He had already lived in Fort Liard for thirty years when we met him in 1985. We would soon learn that he made a welcome practice of exceeding his spiritual mandate.

"You are Catholic?" he asked politely, early into his first visit to our comfortable log home. His accent, thick and French, added music to his voice. I couldn't help wondering how it coloured his Slavey, which he also spoke quite well.

"I was, at one time," I replied hesitantly, not wanting to invoke a theological discussion or an admonition – neither of which was forthcoming, happily.

"Ah, I see," he said with a matter of fact but faintly wistful air. He sat comfortably in a kitchen chair, head back, eyes closed.

"We were married by a United Church minister," I went on, "but truthfully, we don't belong to any church."

"Some are Catholic, some United and some, well, we 'ave all kinds up 'ere, too, you know," he said, smiling. His appearance in conversation was at once both impish and wise but his kind face settled into a resigned and perhaps a somewhat sad expression in quiet moments. A vague, broad white scar marked his lower face and neck. "Somet'ing from de war," is all he is known to have said about it.

One evening in 1986, Father Mary arrived at our door bearing a bulging, green plastic garbage bag. "Do you like chard?" he asked.

"Do we like...?" I wasn't sure I'd heard him correctly.

"Chard," he said again, a little louder, "it's sort of between spinach and celery..."

"Oh, yes, chard! Of course! Yes, we do, actually, like chard," I answered, not sure where this was going. After all, we were north of sixty and this was late September.

"I 'ave more den I can eat and dese people, bless deir 'earts, don't really appreciate good chard. I grow it myself, of course," he said, bustling into the porch.

A slight man, his somewhat stooped profile belied his considerable physical strength and endurance which, together with his patience, faith and temper, had been tried many times by the people and the harsh land. Father Mary was no Sunday afternoon preacher. By the time we had met him, he had traveled the sixty miles of river and bush between his home in Fort Liard and Nahanni Butte, winter and summer, for thirty years bringing the sacraments to his flocks on Sunday.

In the early days he traveled by dog team in the winter, usually following the Liard River from Fort Liard to Nahanni Butte, where it joined the Nahanni River. One such trip took six full days, breaking trail for dogs through snow that was sometimes deeper than he was tall. He would walk ahead for sixty yards, return to the team, mush the sixty yards, then repeat the process. Each night he would build a shelter, keep a fire and cook his own and his dogs' food. This in a land where forty below zero was not uncommon. After the spring break-up he would travel by boat, dodging ice-floes and sandbars. He could replace a propeller shear-pin in mid-river as fast as most people could shout "Help!" It was said no one knew that stretch of the river better than he did.

The inhabitants of the area paid him the highest compliment when they said, "Father Mary can live off the land." Game was scarce in that part of the north and the old saying, "You can't eat the scenery," was an ironic truth. No one knew better than Father Mary that the mountains, forests and rivers, although truly beautiful, hid great dangers.

"Den 'ere you are, lots of chard!" he said, handing over the garbage bag, overflowing with the green vegetable. He looked at me intently. "Do you know 'ow to cook it?"

"Well," I began.

"Just steam it and den add a little butter and salt. Easy," he volunteered.

Father Mary had no more trouble surviving in the kitchen and garden than he did in the bush. Surprisingly, many vegetables grew very well in the north. Father Mary had perfected the northern garden, so much so that the *National Geographic* had featured him in his garden in a 1972 issue.

"You 'ave a plane I understand?" he asked later as we finished the last of a pot of tea.

"Guilty as charged," I responded, always happy to talk airplanes, "it's just a little 172, but we like it."

"A plane makes good sense up 'ere," he said. "At one time I wished to take my licence but my Superior, 'e would not permit it. I'm sure 'e 'ad good reasons, of course!" he quickly added. However, it was clear from his inflection that in obeying his Superior he had been bowing more to his vow of obedience than to the logical weight of argument.

"It would 'ave been perfect for me, of course," he said, wistfully, "especially now, when I must also go to Trout Lake as well as Nahanni and Liard. But I am too old for such t'ings as planes..."

After a few more Sunday evening visits and a deluge of produce from his amazing garden, we grew even more fond of this little priest and looked forward to his weekly visits. But winter was coming and Father Mary was no longer a young man. His health had begun to fail.

"Pilots are always looking for an excuse to fly," I said, casually, one Sunday evening as he gratefully dug into a moose stew.

"Please, take no offence," he said carefully, after a few bites, "but you do not 'ave to cook de moose quite so long. Moose can be very tender if you cut it correctly before you cook it." He looked up, innocently, "An excuse to fly you were saying, excuse me?"

"Well, yes," I took up the topic once more, although I had yet to be convinced moose could be tender. Eventually I did learn how to cook it and Father was quite right. We soon became addicted to moose meat and would hoard it in our freezer when we were lucky enough to get it. "I would be quite happy to fly down to Fort Liard on Sundays and bring you here, if that would suit you."

"Oh, dat would be a lot of trouble, really," he protested, wiping his mouth with his napkin. Yet, he was clearly tempted by the idea. "If you could," he ventured, "I would gladly pay for your gasoline."

84

"I would be happy to," I responded, "and, of course, everything would depend on the weather."

"De wedder, of course," he nodded, smiling while he savored the idea.

As the Bible said, "And so it came to pass" that I was called to the radiophone in the store to take a call from the good father.

"Jim, 'allo, it is Fa'der Mary 'ere!" the unmistakable voice crackled through the static and whistle of the infernal device. "If you wish, you could pick me up on Sunday at Liard. Will you come alone, over?"

" I can. Why do you ask?" I answered.

"Well, I 'ave some t'ings to bring back to Nahanni, if we can get dem in de plane..."

"No problem. I'll see you Sunday," I said, wondering what the cargo might be.

Sunday dawned crisp and clear. By noon I was climbing out over the frozen Liard River, a freshly frozen white snake below UPX's left wing. To my right, the forbidding, snow-capped mountains marched southward to Fort Liard. As I casually surveyed the river, I noticed some dark shapes on the snow-covered ice and instinctively turned and began a descent to investigate. Closer now, I recognized a wolf-kill and leveled off at five hundred feet, not wanting to frighten the pack. Even from this altitude the size of the wolves was impressive and sobering, and as I added power to climb out and turn back on course, the hungry animals barely looked up from the bloody moose carcass that stained the virgin snow. Wildlife was scarce indeed and that was one of the few sightings of any kind I witnessed in all the time I flew those skies.

VFR navigation could be quite easy in that part of the north. Finding Fort Liard was as easy as following the river, which curved past the village, perched on its banks. Or, I could shadow the east side of the mountains southward to the final peak of the chain, a stone's throw from this most southerly of western NWT settlements. Of course, on a clear day, most kinds of flying were easy. I say most, because, although navigation might not have taxed the pilot's abilities in those parts, clear air turbulence was more than a page of theory in the text book.

Like many new northern aviators, I had been rendered a babbling basket case by mountain waves, formed as the westerlies blew across the range and churned the air in their lee to an invisible pitching ocean. These frightening meteorological freaks were nearly invisible except for the peculiar lenticular clouds that perched above the ridge, motionless, like flying saucers. Simultaneously forming and evaporating in the low pressure pockets created by the howling winds along the trailing edges of the mountain ridges, lenticulars meant trouble. I recalled the first time I'd encountered a mountain wave.

"What is going on here?" I'd shouted to an empty cockpit. My seatbelt straining, an invisible force pulled me toward the roof and the altimeter unwound like a windmill, fifteen hundred feet per minute, down! And I was in level flight! I slammed the throttle to the stops, hauled the elevator back and noted, perspiration now fogging my glasses, that the rate of climb indicator was still pinned, down. Just as I was picturing Mary and Johnny at my funeral, wham, UPX hit bottom and immediately began climbing at fifteen hundred, then two thousand feet per minute. What a ride!

I learned to stay a healthy distance from the rocks, where severe turbulence could make an airplane do unnatural acts, and just ride the wave out. Up six thousand feet, down six thousand feet, as unnerving as the ride could be, it was best to just keep steady power on, a level attitude and wait it out.

This same wind created truly interesting landings. More than once I'd approached both the Liard and Nahanni strips sideways. I was secure, if not comfortable, in the knowledge that the effects would be considerably milder once I was in ground effect. I knew that a solid kick to full rudder would make for an acceptable landing — one you could walk away from, that is.

Fort Liard appeared to my right, a scattering of buildings pressing against the river's edge. I scanned the mountain peaks. No lenticulars today but the wind was picking up. I felt a few sharp buffets as I lined up for the generous gravel strip that bounded the south side of the village. No sweat. I could have balanced a dime on its edge on my yoke until touchdown. Wheeling into the ramp, I noticed Father Mary was waiting.

"I don't know if it will be possible, but..." he said, by way of greeting, as he peered into the back seat area of the plane, "I promised one of your citizens I would bring dis stove up to her."

"Stove?" I asked, startled by the suggestion. Of course, I knew that Father Mary often carried more than the scriptures to his far-flung flock. As all their supplies had to be flown in, the freight charges pushed prices at the stores in Nahanni Butte and Trout Lake into the stratosphere. I once paid seventeen dollars for two packages of celery! Hence, the good folks of these communities had come to rely on their pastor's access to the outside world to help bring them the necessities of life. His Sunday trips always included cartage of snowmobile and "kicker" parts, groceries and on occasion, it seemed, stoves.

"It's just a tin stove, but perhaps too big?" he suggested.

"Let's have a look," I said, not at all certain this would be possible.

It was. As we climbed out westward over the Liard into a rising wind, I glanced back to check and to convince myself that we were doing this. Sure enough, strapped and bundled to protect the windows and headliner, a great, black stove occupied the rear passenger seat. Father's substantial army-style rucksack took whatever room was left. Major home appliances had now been added to the growing list of what a 172 could carry.

The stall horn let loose some short, shrill squawks as Papa X-Ray negotiated the increasingly turbulent air. As we rounded the mountain across from the settlement and headed north, I gave it a wide berth. Whump! Now the wind *was* blowing. The first lenticulars had started to form over the rocks as Nahanni's faint gray strip came into view. Whump! Another gust. With one hand firmly clenched around the hand-hold above his door, Father Mary gazed intently ahead at the impossibly narrow Nahanni strip. Surely it was set far too close to the forest pushing in on both sides. Too narrow, too short. His lips were moving. Prayer, or a nervous tic?

Prayer never hurts, but this was my home strip and I knew its limitations well. We approached sideways and rode the gusts down to the treetops. Just as I had expected, the gusts disappeared as I kicked right rudder, dropped below the trees and onto the gravel. Piece of cake. Father Mary smiled and gave me a look of gentle respect. "Perfect!" he proclaimed. I thanked him and didn't argue. Low-timers like me accepted all the compliments we could get.

After school the next day we were piling back into Papa X-Ray, minus the stove. "I always wanted to go to Trout Lake," I assured him, after agreeing to ferry him to the settlement located about one hundred miles southeast of Nahanni.

"You're sure?" he asked, sincerely.

"Really," I said, "I'd like to buy some fish and I'd also like to drop in on a friend of mine who teaches there."

"You will let me pay de gas," he pressed.

"I wouldn't hear of it," I countered. "I just like to fly and I appreciate the company. Now, get in, s'il vous plait!"

After lift-off, I felt a firm prod in my right shoulder. I saw him pointing off to the horizon, to the right of our course. He didn't like to talk in the noisy plane. But Father Mary was not at all shy about offering suggestions regarding our heading. Just as firmly, I pointed to the compass and then straight ahead. He shrugged and pointed again, shouting, "I ground!"

"What?"

"*I ground*! Dat is where Trout Lake is, at de 'igh ground!" he yelled again, pointing to the hills.

I pointed to the heading indicator. "Zero nine zero, that's where it is!" I shouted back. "We can go direct." Another shrug.

Once more a nod, a smile and that look of respect came over his face as we flew, true as a die, straight to Trout Lake.

"Zero nine zero," I shouted, enjoying the moment a little, as we passed over the tiny community clinging to the lip of the lake below. The landing strip must be...where is the landing strip? I wondered to myself.

"Right dere!" he shouted, his hand indicating a line bounding the south side of the village. He read minds, too. Expect miracles, I thought, turning for the unlikely landing area. Final approach. Full flaps, across a small creek, over some wires, past – and I mean right past – the houses, kids and small population. Bump! The wheels touched. A small hill lifted us back into the air, then we were on the ground again, no not quite, one more hill and finally we settled down and pulled to a stop right beside the store.

A three-wheeler roared up and skidded to a stop.

"Hey, Father!" the rider shouted, jumping off the trike. "Let me help you with that!" He took Father Mary's packsack. I stopped him before he could leave.

"Can you tell me where I can buy some fish?"

"I just pulled in my nets. How much do you want?" With that he opened a garbage bag on the back of his trike and started hauling out trout the size of farm animals.

"Wow!" I shouted. "How 'bout five or six, I guess?" He fished out a few big ones while I ran and got the box I'd brought along. As I paid him and put the box in the plane, I noticed one of the fish still flopping. Now that's fresh fish! I thought.

Father Mary and his chauffeur disappeared into the village. It was getting late so I quickly ran to the school to trade shop-talk with its beleaguered master, before launching UPX from the roller-coaster strip and home again.

"See you in a week," I had shouted to Father Mary, whom I'd spied nearby, surrounded by children, on my way to the plane. He waved and nodding deeply, mouthed a thank you.

I logged a dozen or so trips with him that year and my respect for his knowledge, kindness and perseverance grew with each adventure. I was happy to help him with his travels but he insisted on trying to return the favour. In the early part of our third winter, we had occasion to ask for his help, which he immediately obliged.

My Ski-Doo was stranded on the far bank of the frozen Liard, about five miles from Nahanni by the winter road, not yet prepared for the season.

"Could you bring my snowmobile to the village for me?" I asked him by radiophone. "You could come as far as the river by truck and then use my machine to get you to the village this Sunday."

"I am glad to do it," was the instant response.

Sunday evening came and went. He was overdue. After worriedly looking at the clock and then out the window where the temperature had fallen to thirty-five below, Mary said, "I think you should go check it out."

"Nobody knows the bush better than Father Mary," I responded, "especially when snowmobiles are involved. He could do an engine overhaul in the dark in this weather, if he had to."

"But he's late. He'd never leave it this late," she persisted.

"I'll call over to the National Parks Office and see if he went there first, although I doubt he would," I said. I called Doug, the chief warden. He hadn't heard from him. I hung up our radiophone.

"Maybe you should get Raymond and go find..." she stopped suddenly, then shouted, "Oh, my God, there he is!" I ran to the window to see the frosted shape of Father Mary trudging slowly up to the door. As we raced to open the door, the exhausted man, face rimmed with hoar-frost, fell through the doorway and collapsed on a chair.

"I don't know," he said, between breaths, "it just quit on de river and wouldn't run...maybe out of gas, I don't know. I walked."

"The Ski-Doo quit?" I exclaimed. Whatever the reason, the walk had taken its toll. We got him out of his parka and settled him into a kitchen chair. He didn't look well at all.

"How about a little wine?" I offered, uncorking a bottle of the contraband which I kept for medicinal purposes only, of course.

"I am from France," he said through a weak smile. "You do not 'ave to ask a Frenchman if 'e wants a glass of wine!" His hand shaking a little, he took a sip. "Not bad. Is it French?"

"It is now," I answered. He laughed.

This was to be Father Mary's last winter in the north. He began to have trouble with his sense of balance and his strength was failing him quickly. By Christmas he had been sent to France to recuperate. The village welcomed his letters in which he exhorted his people to open their arms and hearts to the new priest who would replace him.

"I am not important," he would write, "it is the message, not the messenger you must remember." For us, the message and the messenger were one and the same.

# Chapter Nine

# White knuckles

Parents and kids alike agreed that the 1986 Christmas concert was an unqualified success. The play was praised as the best ever. Mind you, it was also the first Christmas play ever performed by the students of Charles Yohin School. Santa arrived looking suspiciously like the park warden under the beard and red coat. The green parks-issue trousers gave him away. The Christmas carols were sung and we were gorged with food.

When it was over it was time to get the trip south underway. We had planned to fly Papa X-Ray to Vancouver to spend Christmas with my sister Carol.

"Bad idea," one visiting pilot cautioned. "You shouldn't try to fly the mountains to Vancouver at Christmas time. It's too unpredictable."

"Oh, sure, I've done it," another said, casually. "You have to be careful but it can be done all right."

Mary needed convincing. "It's just a series of short legs," I argued. "You take them one at a time and after all, we've got more than two weeks to get there and back."

"I don't know. They say it's foolish to try this trip in winter."

"We made it to Virginia Falls and back alive," I pleaded.

"We had perfect weather when we did the Virginia Falls trip," Mary reminded me.

"Okay, okay, that's true. But Fred is doing this trip with us," I played my ace. Fred was a bushpilot friend from Fort Nelson who was ferrying a 172 down to Boundary Bay. "He'll be flying ahead of us. What could be safer than having a seasoned guide?"

"Well, I feel better that we're following an experienced pilot so I guess it will be safe enough," Mary offered hesitantly, acknowledging that I had been flying safely and conservatively since I'd received my licence six months earlier. I'd been flying rocks, rivers and bush too, not just Sunday circuits and sightseeing.

91

"We just won't go if the weather is poor this time," I hastened to add.

"If I ever feel like we're in real danger," Mary cautioned, "I'll ask you to turn back."

"I promise," I said, "if you ask me to turn back, I will turn back." It seemed only reasonable. After all, without the confidence of my dear wife and child, flying would become a lonely solo experience. So, even if I knew I had the ability to continue a given flight, she had to agree.

A rule evolved: the pilot's intuition was never allowed to overrule the reason and logic that said, "don't go." However, the copilot's intuition was allowed to overrule the pilot's reason and logic when he argued for going anyway. Transport Canada might call it "flying by the most restrictive rules." The bottom line: if Mary didn't want to go, we didn't go.

6:30 a.m. As usual, the alarm went off in my head a few minutes before the clock radio was set to wake me up. Sliding out of bed, I turned it off before it could ring so Mary wouldn't be awakened. She'd need all the rest she could get. The sun wouldn't be up for more than four hours. At this time of the year, the winter sun barely dropped in for lunch before heading to Florida or wherever it went after disappearing below the mountain-hedged horizon.

I fumbled in the dark for my clothes. Longjohns, two pairs of thick wool socks, pants, shirt and sweater, and then that miracle of modern apparel, the snowmobile suit. I pulled the old navy-blue "Official Ski-Doo" suit over my already well-insulated frame, grateful for successfully resisting Mary's attempts to throw the patched, stitched and grease-stained old friend into the trash. The argument had raged for several years now.

"It's just nicely broken in," I would say, "and remember, your very own mother bought it for me..."

"And she doesn't have to keep patching it up. Really, Jim, how long do you think you can keep on wearing that thing? You've worn it for eleven years already!" And so I started calling it "survival gear". Mary seemed to back off at the word "survival" and the suit became a protected species, which was yet to be retired.

Mukluks, the perfect winter footwear. Elsie Marsellais made mine for me and added a lovely bit of beadwork, no extra charge. The felt-lined beauties slid onto my double-socked feet to complete the picture of the well-dressed northern teacher/pilot. Not small to begin with, I noted that my reflection in the hall mirror resembled something from Mount Rushmore, a face on top of a small mountain.

At forty below, Celsius and Fahrenheit are close enough to shake hands. I noted the temperature as I passed the thermometer, grabbing the little Honda generator on the way out. I plunked it into the home-built sled behind the Ski-Doo. I pulled the starting rope a few times before priming the engine. In spite of arguments from seasoned snowmobilers to the contrary, I just couldn't bring myself to fire up an internal combustion engine at forty below without at least breaking the pistons free. One shot of prime, one pull, and a great cloud of smoke and noise filled the dark morning air.

Dogs barked and howled but no lights appeared in the little log homes that dotted the settlement. Thick columns of smoke rose straight up from their tin stoves in the log houses below. All was serene but for my noisy machine. Trappers often roared out of the village in the wee hours of winter so no one would be bothered by my noisy snowmobile. The black seat cushion was hard as a park bench as I settled down for the short ride to the strip. Glancing back to see that the sled was still there, I roared past the Band Office and the skating rink, toward the woods that led to Papa X-Ray. The headlight flickered and danced over the tree trunks lining the narrow path and came to rest on the airplane sleeping softly under a blanket of new snow. I pulled alongside and cut the engine. I flicked on my flashlight in the unearthly quiet of that cold morning and set about the task of preheating the old Continental O-300 snoozing under its orange thermal cowl cover.

I had devised my own simple, but effective, preheating system. First, I set the generator on a box a few feet from the plane and fired it up. At 40 below the little engine couldn't keep itself warm so I covered it with a cardboard box, enclosing all but the exhaust pipe. If the whole contraption wasn't kept warm, the seals would actually shrink, allowing engine oil to leak out.

Next, I crouched down and slipped a standard electric in-car heater under the lower cowl cover, up through the nosewheel well and into the engine compartment. Finally, I plugged the heater into the generator. The little engine struggled with the load, then its rpms slowly rose again. Good. It was working. I discovered the generator would run exactly three and one-half hours under these conditions, just enough to render the O-300 warm to the touch.

I stood back and checked my work. Glancing at the wings, I noted my makeshift wing covers would make snow removal an easy job later that morning. No point in taking them off now, I knew, as hoar-frost would form again by the time we were ready to leave. I gave the prop tip a tentative pull. Ugh! It wouldn't budge. No question, the engine was forty below, too.

I fired up the Ski-Doo and roared back to the house. I was always amazed at how powerful that machine was and how fast my face froze in the blast of super-cooled air that cleared the windshield. But my trusty suit kept the rest of me warm as toast and only if she happened to touch my nose would Mary know I'd been out of bed as I slid back under the covers to catch the balance of my night's sleep.

The eastern sky started to lighten around ten. By ten-thirty a rosy sunrise announced a crystal-clear morning as I pulled the army-surplus parachute from the wings of Papa X-Ray. The slippery material, laden with snow, required only a gentle tug to send small avalanches plummeting to the growing snowbank behind each wing. Two smaller pieces covered the tail. Just as I bundled the last of the covers into my makeshift shack, a discarded packing crate, the little Honda generator coughed, gasped and died. Perfect timing, I thought, as Mary roared up on the Ski-Doo. Behind her trailed a sled brimming with suitcases, boxes and what appeared to be yet another bundle but turned out to be young Johnny-in-a-snowsuit.

"Got the hang of that thumb-throttle," I commented as I quickly unloaded the sled and dumped in the generator for her to return to the house while I packed up the plane, kid and all.

The temperature had risen to a balmy minus thirty by the time our little family settled into Papa X-Ray's stuffed cabin. I turned the key. As always, the engine fired on the first revolution and quickly settled into a contented purr. I learned not to idle for long as the oil was as likely to get colder as warmer, even with the winter fronts in place. So with checks all done, I taxied out for one-five, cranked her around and eased the throttle to the stops.

At minus thirty, the density altitude was about a thousand feet below sea level and that made for thick air. Papa X-Ray's prop dug into it like a spoon into ice cream and we were airborne with full fuel and a full load, in less than six hundred feet. We rose quickly above the Christmas card scene below, southward, and on to Vancouver.

"I could use that over here," Mary shouted above the engine noise, pointing to my old plastic COPA membership card. I always kept my expired card to scrape the frost that accumulated on the inside of the windshield. As a scraper the card had no equal. Mary wielded it like an expert, scraping the frost off her side.

"Are we there yet, Dad?" The tiny voice proved that there was life under that pile of clothing in the back seat. I glanced over my shoulder at the little face peering out from behind a scarf tied over Johnny's hood. He was breathing on the window and using his finger to melt designs into the frost. His lower body was hidden by a blanket and he was packed on all sides by bags and bundles, more like a wrapped gift than a three-year-old boy.

"Having fun, son?" I laughed, ignoring his famous question.

"Sort of, Dad," came the non-committal reply.

"You're closer to Sandy Lake than usual," said my wife, the Navigator.

"Just look at all those cabins," I said, pointing below, hoping to distract her from the chart glued to her knees.

"Won't it take longer if you don't fly a straight line?"

"Yes, dear," I agreed. A course correction was much easier than a wife correction. I began a gentle turn to the east.

The clear weather stayed with us for the hour-and-a-half flight to Fort Nelson. As Mary supervised the refueling of UPX and the bathroom stop for Johnny, I headed to the Environment Canada office where Fred was waiting for me.

"So, you're ready to go?" he asked, as we leaned on the counter and studied the weather charts. Fred was a can-do kind of guy, a commercial charter operator with thousands of hours of bush-flying experience. He seemed quite upbeat, in spite of what looked like worsening weather in the southern half of B.C.

"I guess it doesn't look too bad for the first leg," I offered.

"There appears to be some weather coming in from the southwest and we may have some trouble down around Prince George but it looks good enough to get started, hey?" Fred said enthusiastically.

"See you in the air," I shot back, heading for the door.

As we climbed out over the bush south of Fort Nelson, I heard Fred departing down below.

"I'll just follow you, Jim," he radioed on 122.9, "and try to stay close enough for visual contact."

"Roger that, Fred." Good, I'd rather be behind him but at least he wouldn't be outrunning me ahead. Although his 172 was newer than ours, there seemed to be little difference in cruise speed and we expected to would be able to stay close together. So, where was he?

"Come in Fred," I called. "Where are you?"

"Yeah, Jim... I'm just crossing the rocks and heading out over Williston Lake, over."

What? He was already over the lake and we were still following the ridge southward. Seemed he was taking a short-cut and if we wanted to keep up we had to jump that ridge pronto.

Never approach a ridge straight on, they always said. I was familiar with that old advice but on this occasion I had more than two thousand feet between my wheels and those rocks, so I headed straight for the ridge, anyway.

"Why are we descending?" Mary asked, more curious than concerned.

"Well, it's the ridge effect," I answered, not concerned but surprised at how fast we were going down. The wind was right on our nose and as it flowed toward us over the mountains ahead, it promptly slid down the near slope, leaving us in a steady downdraft. I added more power, and finally, full power. We cleared the rocks by just under a thousand feet. Not dangerous but interesting. Mental note: don't try this with only a thousand feet to spare.

"May as well stay down here, anyway," I added. "Seems to be some cloud ahead."

"Cloud?" Mary looked up from her chart and scanned our flightpath. Below us a very cold and partially frozen Williston Lake lay in a glittering narrow strip bounded on either side by sheer cliffs offering no possibility for a forced landing. Formed by the Bennet Dam, now below and behind our left wing, Williston Lake was deep and long.

"Say, Fred," I radioed on 122.9, "how's it look up there?"

"Not too bad," came the slightly garbled reply. "There's a bit of scud but the visibility's fine."

"How far up are you?" I asked, noting that the clouds appeared to be a good distance off yet.

"I'm just about..." was all I heard as his transmission faded into garbled static. So much for the buddy system. Chalk up one more hazard of mountain flying. Radios don't broadcast through solid rock very well, and as long as Freddie was around one rocky corner or another, we were all alone. And here comes that cloud.

"I don't like this, Jim," Mary said, now clearly concerned.

"Not to worry," I said feigning more confidence than I felt. "It's just some loose scud and it's not that low. We'll just drop down here and get under it." I descended to about a thousand feet above the water but the clouds ahead still blocked the view. Another five hundred feet and we were under the first of them and now appeared to be in a tunnel. The lower we descended the narrower the lake became until, at two hundred feet above the freezing lake, cloud above and rock cliffs to either side, I tried another call to Fred.

"What do you see up there Fred, come in?" I transmitted.

"How's it going back there?" the welcome response crackled back. It sounded good to hear his voice.

"Well, I'm under that scud and have good visibility. As long as it doesn't get any worse than this we'll be all right, over."

"No, that's as low as it gets. I'm out at the corner now and heading south. There's a bit of snow starting but the ceiling is higher and the visibility is not too bad. I'm going to stop at Mackenzie for fuel."

"Sounds good to me," I radioed back. "See you there." I could feel the tension lift a little as I began a gentle climb toward the higher ceiling ahead. I was beginning to suspect that what was "okay" for a pilot of Fred's experience just might be a bit beyond my own capabilities. Sensing Mary's deteriorating confidence, I patted her knee and said, "Look, as long as we have Fred up front we'll be all right. Don't worry." It sounded good and I might have improved her attitude a bit but then it started to snow.

"There's the bend!" I called out as I began a turn southward along the east side of the lake which, unlike the previous arm, was completely frozen over.

"All I can see is snow on this side," came the nervous response from the right seat. The white frozen lake and the snow below merged into one white canvas on her side.

"Look, it's clear sailing from here," I cajoled, half-believing this myself. "All we have to do is follow the lakeshore for another forty miles or so and we'll hit Mackenzie. It's right on the lake."

The shoreline was easy to follow even as the visibility dropped to three miles, then two and then one. Soon I was looking almost straight down at the shoreline, all the time trying to stay below cloud. My one hundred and fifty hours of experience didn't include instrument flying but I had learned that one can be in visual conditions one second and instrument the next. Look too long at the chart, look up and you're in cloud. And in deep doo-doo. I

97

glanced at the chart that Mary gripped in her white-knuckled hand and could see that not far off to the left were firm, solid mountains not to be trifled with.

"Check the numbers, please," I asked her, handing her the flight supplement and straining to keep calm.

"One twenty-six seven," she responded, her voice now quivering a bit.

I dialed it quickly, not wanting to look away from that precious shoreline. Twenty-six seven? I thought, that was Prince George. How am I supposed to get conditions at Mackenzie when the guy at the other end of the radio is in Prince George?

"Mackenzie radio, Uniform Papa X-Ray, over," I tried.

"Uniform Papa X-Ray, Prince George, go ahead," came the clear reply.

"Prince George, Uniform Papa X-Ray, VFR, approximately ten miles north of Mackenzie landing Mackenzie, request advisory please."

I listened to the advisory and learned little except that Fred had already landed and was waiting for us. Apparently, the conditions weren't great but were do-able. Nothing to do at this point but follow the shoreline and put her down in Mackenzie. Now, where was Mackenzie?

"That looks like something," Mary said, excitedly, pointing to some buildings below on the shoreline.

"Must be it," I said. "Now to find the airport."

"Look for a railroad," Mary said after checking her chart. "Just follow it into town and it goes right by the airport."

"There it is!" I exclaimed to Mary, pointing down to the tracks that appeared to be converging into one line, heading south. "But it looks like we've gone past the town!" The visibility was now deteriorating faster than ever. I descended to five hundred, then three hundred feet, my straining eyes glued to the shoreline.

The alarm went off in my head. Any further and we'd be newspaper headlines tomorrow morning.

"I'm going to have to turn around," I stated as calmly as I could, "and we're going to be IFR while I do it, so I'll need your help. I can't turn to the left because I don't know how close those mountains are. I do know we have lots of room to the right but we'll lose sight of the ground if we turn that way, so you will have to be my eyes, 'cause I'll be glued to the instrument panel."

"Dad! Dad!" Johnny was calling from the back seat, "It's all white out there, Dad!"

That's why they call it a white-out, I thought, and it kills people like us all the time. But there was no time to ponder my stupidity or to even answer my young son, staring out the left rear window at the swirling snow that enveloped us. Greasy with sweat, my left hand was locked in a vice-like grip on the yoke while my right hand nudged the throttle forward as I began the longest one-hundred-and-eighty-degree turn I have ever made, out over the frozen lake, invisible below us in our white cocoon.

Mary, my precious wife and partner, struggled to disguise her panic as she followed my instructions to look for any sign of lake or trees while I held my attention firmly on the instruments. They showed a level fifteen-degree turn — good. And they showed we were three hundred feet above the invisible ice-covered water that would be our final destination if I made yet one more ill-considered decision.

"Are you sure about this?"

Now she was starting to panic and I couldn't blame her. In fact, I wasn't sure. I was, in fact, dead wrong. Never turn out over a frozen lake in conditions like these, I have been told a hundred times since. Once you lose sight of the shoreline you'll have no horizon and then... But no one had ever told me just how to handle this. I'd never heard the proper procedure: turn out toward the lake until the shoreline is just barely visible and then turn back in. Simple. But I was learning a lot today and this was just one of many lessons I'd live to remember.

Johnny was glued to his window, fascinated by the zero visibility. I was one with this machine, not allowing the altimeter to move ten feet let alone a hundred, as this endless turn was the most important I ever had to make in my life. The DG rotated painfully, almost 180 degrees, then...

"Trees! There are some trees!" Mary yelled, not in panic, but drenched with relief. And there it was, that blessed shoreline. I locked onto it, dialed in the ADF and headed for that beacon, which turned out to be less than a mile away. The airfield materialized right below us out of the swirling snow and my eyes never left it until our wheels touched the white-covered asphalt and we all breathed aloud.

The rest of the flight to Vancouver was perfect, smooth and fast. We chatted and enjoyed each other's company while we lunched on snacks. Even Johnny loved it.

"See," I said to Mary, tucking into lunch as we cleared the coastal range and headed into Vancouver, "it's no big deal."

"Would you like some wine with your meal, sir?"

"I don't drink and fly as a rule," I responded, "but I believe I'll have some. Yes, I'll have some wine." And with that the flight attendant poured an airline-sized bottle of Pacific Western Airlines red into my waiting glass. As I leaned back in my seat, I looked over at Johnny and Mary in the seats next to me, joking and laughing and very much alive. On course from Prince George to Vancouver, the Boeing 737 rolled into a gentle right turn above the snowy peaks hidden in the dark night below.

# Chapter Ten

# Time ex'd

In the spring before I learned to fly in Papa X-Ray, Greg and I were leaning up against the old school by the riverbank, slapping mosquitoes and talking airplane engines. Since they carried him above the unforgiving rocks, bush and water, Greg took airplane engines seriously. I hung on every word of experience he would drop on me.

Greg was a working bush pilot. A sandy-haired man in his thirties, he ferried his wife and two children into Nahanni every spring. He'd settle into his big log house on the northern edge of the village and start getting ready for his clients. His exclusive outfitting business attracted well-heeled hunters from around the world to pit their wits against the caribou and Dahl sheep that roamed the upper Nahanni. We'd get to spend some time with Greg at the tail end of one school year and the front end of the next. Then he'd head back south to Alberta for the winter, taking his two planes with him.

A pretty yellow Piper Super Cub was Greg's pride and joy. With its big fat tundra tires looking like Mickey Mouse ears, Greg could land that cub just about anywhere from sand bars to mountain meadows, and he probably did, more than once. In the spring and fall we would often look up to see the yellow Cub arc northward, ferrying supplies to camps high in the mountains.

As the new owner of an aircraft but having no licence or flying experience to date, I needed to learn fast. I knew that Papa X-Ray's Continental engine had to be overhauled at 1800 hours. The logbook showed 1550. That left 250 hours to major overhaul time and I was trying to figure out how long it would take me to arrive at those magic numbers — the numbers that made cash disappear like magic!

"You'll have to fly a lot to fly a hundred hours a year," Greg mused. "Most private pilots don't do half that much flying. You should get two and a half years at that rate. But you might get three or more..." Greg did well to disguise his pity for the poor fool who was eating up his every word.

He had meant well but Greg was as wrong as Pat Boone in a punk band. Not long after that conversation I took my licence in Papa X-Ray during the summer and flew her home to Nahanni Butte with seventy-five hours left on the clock. Then there was the trip to Virginia Falls, a few trips to Fort Liard, Fort Nelson and...I was down to twenty hours. I had owned a plane for less than ten months and already I was facing my first major overhaul. My wallet started to ache. I began to think bad thoughts about Greg.

Two and a half years? It took me less than ten months to fly those two hundred hours and that was before Christmas! "Well, I guess you're flying more than an average private pilot!" Greg would probably say. And then he'd smile that sly smile that said, "Wanna fly your own plane? Get out your wallet, buddy!" But now, Greg was tucked into his winter home a thousand miles to the south and well out of earshot.

When Papa X-Ray's generator packed it in one winter day, early in '87, I left the plane in Fort Nelson for a week to get refitted. I hitched a ride down to pick it up and took the occasion to raise the dreaded subject with Wade, the local mechanic at Northstar Aviation.

"Well," he began, "they've got a new thing now, Transport Canada does. It's called 'on-condition'." I was staring at him with big banjo eyes. My mind was racing. My wallet had stopped throbbing. "You might be able to take the engine past overhaul."

"Might?" I asked, hopefully. "What are the conditions for going on-condition?"

"Does she use any oil?"

"Hardly any," I replied, truthfully, my heart leaping expectantly at the prospect of squeezing yet more service out of the trusty O-300D.

"Well," he continued, "under the new rules, if you kept good records of oil and fuel consumption and if the compression was okay, and if it passed a Borescope inspection..."

"Borescope?" This was a new word. And I liked it.

"Yeah, it's a neat little tool that lets you look into the cylinders and check for cracks and wear..."

"I don't think I have any cracks, do you?"

"Don't know. I'd hafta look — with a Borescope." He sat on the edge of his desk.

"I like the sound of this," I enthused, "so I guess I'll bring her in around Easter. It'll be due for the next hundred hour then and you can do the, um…"

"Borescope inspection," Wade finished for me. "Sure, Jim, we can do that. But don't get your hopes too high. There are reasons why Continental set the TBO at 1800 hours, you know."

An eternal, insufferable optimist (according to my wife), I didn't hear that part. Mentally, I was figuring that Papa X-Ray's powerplant seemed to be performing just fine, used little oil and sounded healthy. So I paid my bill and left, hopes high that I might stave off the dreaded major that now loomed only twenty hours of flying away.

Wade had parked UPX down the ramp a piece beside a hangar. I had brought my survival gear along for the trip back. I piled it outside the door of the nearby Esso for easy access. Then I popped in to see Hughie and pay my fuel bill before setting out to retrieve Papa X-Ray.

Once again, it was winter in the north and the sun was hurtling toward the horizon where it liked to set around mid-afternoon. Since I had no night endorsement and since Nahanni's strip wasn't lit, I figured I'd better get going. I found Papa X-Ray under a blanket of snow, unlocked it and began my walk-around. First, the snow had to be brushed off and the plane had to be hauled out of the corner of the lot. Time ticked away.

I climbed on each strut and peeked into each tank. Full, I noted, then pulled the prop through a few blades and walked around to check the oil. What the...? No oil? Can't be right, I thought, plunging the dipstick in for another check. I pulled it out and stared at the clean silvery metal. No question, there's no oil in this engine. I glanced at the sun, now plunging toward the horizon, and my pace picked up to a fast jog back to the Esso.

"Oil," I explained, slightly out of breath, "eight litres of multigrade. I guess the guys wanted to keep me on my toes, eh?" I laughed as Hughie handed over the oil.

"You figure?" he asked, a little skeptical.

"Well, when they pulled that generator they had to drain the oil and when they put the generator back on there was no good reason to run the engine up so they just hauled it over and tied it down, without checking the oil. But that's not their fault, right? It's up to the pilot to check the oil before flying..."

"And I guess you just found out why that's so important, eh?" A new voice joined the conversation. He was a commercial pilot friend of mine who was lounging in the FBO, waiting for a late passenger.

"Sure did!" I noted the time. "I guess you're anxious to get going, eh?" I suggested.

"Not really," he replied, "you can't be in a rush when you fly. It's cheaper to spend the night in a hotel than in the bush. Hard to do, not to rush." He turned the page of his magazine, letting slip a small smile.

"Gotta go! Bye!" I said, racing out the door with the oil.

In went the oil. I'll take the empties with me and save time, I thought, as I strapped myself in. Six shots of prime, no time for fooling around and, hmmm, the primer doesn't feel quite right. Mags on, full rich and there she goes, right on the first revolution. I glanced left to check the oil pressure just starting to come up when it abruptly dropped to zero. I wasn't surprised because the engine had just stopped running. "What the heck is going on here?" I said out loud, once again eyeing the sun, now in free-fall straight down. More prime. Still feels funny. Once again I turned the key and once again the engine started and yes, once again it stopped.

Salty language ricocheted through the cockpit. As a farmboy in Saskatchewan I had learned long ago that swearing helped with machinery. I know, I suddenly realized, she's frozen up! Sure enough, I thought, they had it in the warm hangar, the ice crystals in the fuel tanks melted and when they pulled it outside the water froze the fuel lines shut! Now at a full gallop, I headed once again for the Esso.

"Alcohol," I panted, "and lots of it."

"Fuel lines frozen?" My pilot friend looked up at me over his glasses.

"Yeah," I shot back, then was out the door and back to the plane, frost now forming around my sweating face as I dumped the methyl hydrate into the tanks. Back in the plane, prime... still feels weird. I turned the key and, nothing! Nothing?

"More gas-line alcohol," I panted after I'd raced once more to the little building and its reclining occupant, now more than a little amused at my predicament.

"How do you know she's froze?" he asked, putting down his magazine.

"Well, it's just not getting any fuel," I answered, out of breath and exasperated.

104

"Sounds like it might be frozen up right at the old fuel selector," he offered, examining his hands. His broad hint hung in the air for a long moment before it landed on my cerebral cortex. The red glow started at my mukluks, rose through the snowmobile suit and crept up my neck. It was reaching my face as I bolted from the Esso, the new energy in my step fired by embarrassment more than adrenaline. The fuel selector! Good God almighty! Of course!

Sure enough, relief and embarrassment soon gave way to anger at my own stupidity as I looked down and saw the fuel selector lever pointing to OFF. Of all the amateurish things I'd done this took the cake! Of course, there was a reason I'd made the mistake but it was no better than the mistake itself. I rarely turned the fuel off so I had gotten into a habit of checking it only after the engine was running, as part of my pre-takeoff check.

With an uninhibited supply of 80 octane now coursing through the carburetor, the O-300 purred happily as I pulled out onto the ramp calling the tower controller for an advisory on the go. A glance at the sun and my watch then a quick calculation – yup! I'd have just enough time to get home before dark. Just. I had to taxi right past the Esso where I averted my eyes, embarrassed, and I headed right to the end of two-five for a run-up.

I could make it home before sundown, if I didn't get held up one more time, I thought. The run-up was perfect and in a few minutes I was climbing out over the frozen timber and muskeg and banking north toward the distant butte and home.

Finally, I thought, I'm under way at last. My heart slowed to a more relaxed tempo and I adjusted the cabin heat to my well-insulated body. The snowmobile suit made a great flight-suit and the mukluks were comfortable and warm. Yes sir, I was prepared. Why, with the way I was dressed and with the axe, the sleeping bag and the tent in my survival kit. My survival kit?

I didn't even have to look to know it wasn't in the plane. I knew exactly where it was. It was piled neatly outside the door of the Esso where I didn't see it because I deliberately looked away. This really was getting to be too much. Don't rush. Easy to say, hard to do. Too late to go back, I headed over to follow the Liard highway, the only refuge for a pilot with no survival gear should his tired old engine decide to quit. I kept a sharp ear tuned to that engine for the balance of the trip home.

To its credit, the little Continental just hummed right on through the spring, till Easter. The snow melted away and so did the last few hours of engine time. I dropped it at Northstar, time ex'd, checked into a motel and waited hopefully. The Borescope would tell all. The phone rang. It was Wade at Northstar.

"She's toast. You've got next to no compression and three cracked cylinders…"

"Other than that?" I tried a little humour.

"Other than a major overhaul, she looks good," Wade returned, laughing. Ugh. I felt a large stab of pain in my wallet.

Oh, well, it had to happen sometime, I thought to myself. And, look on the bright side, I continued to the same captive audience, you'll get a brand new engine out of the deal. Resigned to my fate, I ordered up the overhaul and eight weeks later I took a call by radiophone from Wade.

"How much?" I asked. The international question that can solve almost any problem.

"Are you sitting down?" he asked. They love to say that, those aircraft mechanics, I thought. They know they have us by a tender part of our nether extremities. They know we're addicted to airplanes and that we'll pay anything to get our precious babies back, well, maybe not anything, but…

"How *much*?" I wasn't enjoying this banter. He told me.

"That much, huh?" It was anticlimactic. It was bang on the estimate and that's all I wanted to know. Now I sat down.

"So, how'd it run up?" I asked.

"Ran up good."

"Safe to fly it over the bush?"

"Don't see why not."

"Okay. You fly, right? How'd you like to fly it up here?"

"Glad to."

I liked an engineer who wouldn't ask me to do anything he wouldn't do himself.

The next day, just before noon, Papa X-Ray appeared coming out of the sun flying sideways into a howling westerly Chinook. I joined several squinting Nahanni-ites who were following its progress downwind for one five. That sound was my new engine, all throaty and powerful. It was in the hands of a pilot whose crosswind landing skills were, umm, come to think of it, unknown to me. I stood nervously by the store watching him bring it around to the base leg.

"Your plane?" old George asked, joining my review of the proceedings.

"Yeah, I'm just getting it back after the overhaul," I replied. "The mechanic's flying it in — or trying to." The little 172 was all over the place as Wade tried to line it up to the south. It was as good a choice as any since the wind was blowing straight across, hard. It was playing those cute little games I had grown to fear and respect in my year of flying these parts.

Doesn't look good from here, I thought, and I guess it didn't look good from up there either as I heard my new engine rev to full power as Wade elected to go around for another try.

A small crowd had now gathered, all watching with detached interest to see how, or whether, I would get my plane back in one piece.

"Taking him a while," Jimmy said, casually.

"He can stay up there until the fuel runs out and I don't mind," I answered calmly, "as long as he gets it down eventually and doesn't roll it into a ball." My armpits were getting damp.

Here he comes again, looking good this time, yes, he's down and now he's out of sight behind the trees and nope, no loud noises. Wade taxied into the village and stepped out. Papa X-Ray was home.

"Interesting wind you have here," Wade said, his voice betraying none of the tension he must have felt earlier.

"How'd she run?" I asked.

"Like a top," he responded, and added, laughing, "not that I had any doubts, eh?"

"Of course not Wade. You installed it, right?" I laughed with him, as I popped the inspection cover and admired the gleaming new engine. "Welcome home, baby," I muttered.

# Chapter Eleven

# 24-hour VFR

When the ice bridge across the Liard was completed the previous Christmas, we set out to rescue our 1977 GMC Sierra Classic pickup from the Department of Public Works compound in Fort Simpson. We thought we could get some use out of it in Nahanni, where trucks were rarities.

It was beautiful, for a truck, complete with canopy, one-ton springs, ten-ply tires and tire chains, cruise control and 454 thirsty cubic inches of displacement. Mary and I hitched a ride to Fort Simpson, fired up the faithful vehicle and headed for the Butte. We tuned in CBC radio and set off across the first ice bridge of the trip, a curving half-mile or so across the Liard River at Fort Simpson. We veered right at The Junction and pointed her shiny nose south; cruise control set for the legal maximum and maybe a bit more, a blast of white powdered snow marking our passage.

Travelers were rightfully wary of this road, stretching hundreds of miles south to Fort Nelson, British Columbia. There were but a handful of humans within walking distance either side of the road along its entire span. One could easily have frozen to death in a disabled vehicle before anyone happened along to help. More than one stranded driver had burned his spare tire to stay alive and warm on that highway. But it was a good road, especially in winter, and spectacular.

Unlike the winters of central and coastal Canada, the winters of the prairies, though often cold in the extreme, were not dreary. We'd learned that the Fort Simpson area was a northern geological extension of the flat prairies to the south. (Maybe that's why it feels so familiar, I wondered, recalling my prairie roots). Brilliant blue skies were the norm, rather than the exception, and the days, although startlingly short, were usually resplendent with glittering snow and diamond-peaked mountains. The white landscape reflected and intensified the winter sun which now hung low on the horizon.

"Blackstone coming up," Mary announced. "Do you want to drop in on Edwin and Sue?"

"Not today," I answered, "we'd better make some tracks for home. It's late."

You could blink and miss the entrance to the homestead at Blackstone, just a few miles from the winter road to Nahanni. The handful of trappers and loggers who called this idyllic spot on the Liard River home included Vera Turner, widow of the legendary trapper, aviator and author, Dick Turner. Dick and Vera had arrived here in the twenties and never returned to their southern roots, preferring to put down new ones in their adopted northern home. Vera's long-time friends, Edwin and Sue Lindberg, now kept Blackstone alive and thriving, always extending warm hospitality to each fresh crop of bushy-tailed and usually green southerners.

A widening of the road past Blackstone marked an emergency airstrip, one of several along the highway. Landing there was always risky, as you could roll out into the radiator of a Mac truck. It was, after all, an emergency strip and inbound pilots were well-advised to have evidence of some sort of emergency if the RCMP happened along. Oil-splattered cowlings helped in such a situation.

"Nahanni Butte", the sign said, as we turned off onto the winter road. It offered a drive through the illustrations of a story book. I stopped to install the tire chains for the balance of the trip. I had a big engine and good tires but only two-wheel drive. Too bad I'm not a condo dweller in Toronto, I thought, I'd have a four-by-four for sure! I inspected the chains, checking their tension, then climbed back in and headed into the bush, tire chains tinkling merrily aft.

"This is so beautiful," Mary said, wistfully, "I wish we'd get out into the bush a bit more, instead of always flying over it." Mary was on a mission to explore her immediate environment, no matter where we lived. A good mission, to be sure, but one not shared by her spouse – not wholeheartedly, at least.

"Well, you're welcome to take this old truck for a ride any time you want," I replied. And I meant it. Although she would not attempt to fly a plane, Mary had been driving more years than me and she loved the truck.

"All right, I will," she smiled. This being the only road in or out, I wondered where she might explore. But I saved that thought.

The one-lane trail snaked through tall timber and muskeg, impassable in warmer months, it was now firm with the winter frost. Deep snow lay in thick blankets on fallen logs, undisturbed by wind that brushed only the tops of the tall spruce, pine and birch trees. Around one more bend, down a natural bobsled hill and there lay the Liard River, a half-mile wide and forbidding as an ice-fall on Everest.

"Ooooooohh!" Mary let go an involuntary expression of awe and trepidation. "I hope it's as solid as they say!"

It was a formidable sight. Chunks of ice the size of railroad cars reared up from the frozen river, trapped for the winter months in their last movement as the cold overtook their passage north-ward. By contrast, true as a die, the ice bridge stretched out across the hostile terrain, marked on either side by carefully placed, miniature spruce trees.

"Not to worry," I assured her, "they took a caterpillar across first so I think we're okay with this truck."

"Yeah, but they lose a caterpillar every now and then too," she shot back. I turned to her, took her hand and looked her in the eye, trying to look as serious as I could.

"It is a good day to die!" I said. Then I gunned the engine, laughed and checked the rear-view mirror to see the snow kicked up by my chains. I slowed immediately, not wanting to tempt fate and to keep to the recommended speed – which was supposed to be varied. Something about not setting up a rhythm that could vibrate to create a crack, I'd heard. But that could have been just beer-talk.

Not so much as a crack or creak betrayed our crossing, though I was grateful for the chains and the big engine as we climbed the steep embankment on the other side, the wheels spraying dirt and snow back onto the pristine river ice.

"Whoooeeee!" Mary shouted as we cleared the bank and turned left. She liked this kind of stuff. Five miles later the Butte appeared from behind a stand of birch, reflecting the golden or-ange of the mid-afternoon sunset. A little farther and rising rib-bons of smoke appeared in advance of the settlement itself. Dogs barked and the children rushed out to see the first vehicle of the season. Until now, the only permanent vehicle in the settlement, other than the Cat, was Duffy's truck. Even more battered since it had hauled our cargo in from the strip on our first day in Nahanni, it always managed another day, month and year of hesitant service as taxi, tractor and general hell-raiser. Now there was another truck. I swung the shiny modern critter, chains jingling, around our log house and brought it to rest on the south side facing the store.

And there it sat, months later, when... "How much do you want for your truck?"

"It's not for sale."

"How much do you want?" Jimmy repeated, without emphasis. The Slavey People of the western Northwest Territories could not have been farther removed from the grand bastions of capitalism to the south but no one understood the basic principles of supply and demand better than these quiet, thoughtful and resourceful people.

"Really, Jimmy, I don't want to sell this truck," I answered, exasperation creeping into my voice.

I had the nicest-looking truck in Nahanni Butte and it was attracting a tire-kicker. The fact that it was not for sale seemed to be of little concern to Jimmy. Trucks could be very useful in the winter, as airplane charters were an expensive proposition at any time. For the price of a charter trip by Cessna 206 or 185 from Nahanni to Fort Simpson and back, a distance of some two hundred air miles return, one could buy a commercial airline ticket to Europe from Edmonton, Vancouver or Toronto. But, in Fort Simpson, one could visit friends and relatives and spend a day or two in the local licensed taverns. A trip to Europe would have paled by comparison. Nope. Luxury was a truck, not an exotic vacation. For, although Nahanni had no access by road nine months of the year, that precious winter road was an important link between the isolated settlement and the outside world.

He was back. "How much do you want for the truck?" Jimmy asked, his inflection unchanged from the first time he'd raised the question. All right, I thought, you want this truck, really want this truck?

"Well, Jimmy," I began, resigned to his determination, "I want what it's worth to me and that's more than most people would want to pay for it. I know this truck. I know it will give years more reliable service in spite of its age and mileage. That's why I don't want to sell it."

"How much?" he persisted, undaunted by my logic. I paused long and hard, a strategy I had picked up from these people more by osmosis than design, then I told him my price, evenly, expecting him to finally back off.

"Okay," was all he said.

"Okay what?" I asked.

"Okay, I'll buy it," he answered, his tone still flat. I looked at the truck, then at Jimmy. "I'll give you five hundred now and the rest later," he added, "if that's all right?" We shook on it.

I knew he was good for the money. Jimmy was a newcomer to Nahanni, a resident by marriage. He had lived in bigger places than this and had experience with machinery, carpentry and with trucks. His talents made him very employable and he stayed busy. But he would need a bank loan to augment his cash and this would mean a trip to Fort Simpson. Well, we were in no rush and neither was Jimmy, in spite of his dogged determination to cut a deal in the first place.

When spring arrived and the ice started to soften, Mary and I took the winter road as far as Blackstone to Edwin's place where we parked the two-toned object of Jimmy's desire. He would pick it up there in June when we would close the deal. As this truck passed from our hands, we knew we were severing yet one more tie with the music business. But we didn't need a truck any more, we had Papa X-Ray and what better way to get Jimmy to his bank loan appointment in Simpson, late in June?

The wind was blowing the afternoon we took off and when the wind blew hard, it blew from the west. At Nahanni, the full fury of the Chinook could really be felt, which was why we departed sideways, weather-cocking into the westerly as soon as my wheels left the gravel on one-five. With thirty knots on the tail at 3,500 feet, we crossed the field at Fort Simpson less than an hour after takeoff.

The windsock indicated that we had our choice of landing direction. Either way, the wind was blowing at right angles to the runway. I chose the usual way in, from the south. Strong crosswinds always induced a pucker-factor, but the stand of bush that lined the western side of the town airstrip created truly interesting turbulence that added new dimensions to the experience.

"Hang on," I said to my passenger, "this isn't going to be pretty." My words fell on deaf ears. No one needed to tell Jimmy to hang on. For a Slavey he was looking unusually Caucasian, especially the knuckles on his right hand which were locked in a death grip on the handle above his door.

I came in hot, left wing low and the rudder to the stops. I didn't care that this wasn't going to be one to be proud of but I had a passenger who needed to get to his bank alive. I opted to use the full 3,000 feet. Wham! The left wheel hit and three-fifths of a second later a wicked gust drove us back into the air. No problem. I'd have said "no sweat" but my damp armpits would have betrayed me. Determined now, I had my eyes on the end of the strip and I was going down that centre line one way or another, even if I was ten feet above it. Two more contacts with earth and we were on the ground weaving back and forth. I continued to fight for control and won. "You can relax now," I said to Jimmy. "We may go off the end but I'm pretty sure we'll live."

For all that he didn't seem much bothered by the landing, even though it was his first time flying with me. We chatted about other things as we walked up to the Simpson Air office.

There were two charter operations in Fort Simpson, Wolverine Air and Simpson Air. Both companies were owned and operated by the gentlest of kind folk and both regularly welcomed me to park on their respective properties. I alternated, not wanting to take their hospitality for granted, and gratefully stayed at one or the other on each trip.

"Hey, Jim," Paul called out. "Breezy huh? What's that stain on the back of your pants?"

"Grease from the landing!" I laughed.

We said our hellos to everyone there and, of course, everyone knew everyone else. Jimmy and I wasted no time. The bank would close soon and we needed to take care of the loan.

At eleven o'clock that same evening I was dozing in the plane, waiting for Jimmy. The bank had gone smoothly. I was merely there to provide information about the truck, not to help with the loan. Jimmy's credit was good. We had separated after we left the bank. I had some business to attend to at the Department of Education and he had to meet some friends.

"Eleven o'clock at the plane, okay?" I had asked as we parted.

"Okay," he said, "eleven o'clock."

But there was no sign of Jimmy. I wasn't too surprised. Agreed times were more elastic in the north. I lived the same way. Besides, the wind hadn't let up and there was no way I was going to try landing at Nahanni with this wind blowing. So I was happy to wait. In late June the sun never really set. It was a magical time for aviators, officially 24-hour VFR. Commercial flights in single-engine planes operated day and night since there was no real night. I was looking forward to the experience of flying at night however light it was.

I phoned Mary. "The wind's still blowing," she said, "and it looks like it's still straight out of the west. I wouldn't try landing in this."

"I'll wait 'til one o'clock and if it's stopped, I'll leave, Jimmy or no," I said. I decided to sack out in Papa X-Ray. With the seat reclined full back, I settled in, content and as comfortable as only an owner could be in his own airplane on such a night. The wind rocked me to sleep.

What was that? I sat up, momentarily disoriented and checked my watch. One o'clock. The wind had stopped. I was awakened by the silence. I checked the ramp. No sign of Jimmy. Oh, well, enough is enough, I thought. He'd got the loan and the truck deal was done. Guess he's just celebrating. I decided to leave without him.

Ten minutes later I climbed Papa X-Ray over the town and into a perfect sky, glowing in the brief rosy northern twilight between sunset and sunrise. I flicked on my red panel light and felt more important as the cockpit took on the red glow of an airliner. Hmmm. I'm going to enjoy flying at night when I get my endorsement this summer, I thought. I dialed up Flight Service and filed a flight plan for the Butte.

The muskeg and Antoine Lake passed placidly below me and the Liard wound its way toward me, northeastward, off to my left. Blackstone was coming up. Bump! What was that? Bump-bump! Another one! What the heck? Turbulence! My heart sank as I realized that the wind was still blowing here. How the heck could the wind be blowing so hard here with not a breath of the same only fifty miles behind me in Fort Simpson?

I didn't think of turning back. After all, it was technically daylight and it couldn't be blowing as hard in Nahanni as it had been earlier. Not now, not at one-thirty in the morning! Right?

Wrong. As the Butte approached on my right, the mountain and its sisters behind it churned the racing air into an unruly beast. It wasn't until I rounded the corner into the shade of the Butte that the other problem surfaced.

Even in the dim light, the mountains lying to the north of Nahanni cast a black shadow. I could just make out the houses of the village and the gray landing strip beyond. It's almost certainly blowing straight across, I thought, so it doesn't matter which way I come in. I'll cross over and check the flag at the school. There it is! Stiff as frozen long johns and pointing straight east, straight across three-three, one-five.

I turned right for a right-hand to one-five but Papa X-Ray didn't seem to want to turn around. The wing kept wanting to go all the way over. Can't keep going in this direction. There's the "little butte" out here somewhere too, I reminded myself, ready to eat me like a can of corned beef.

The little butte, a fifteen-hundred-foot sheer rock outcrop, rose to the west of the strip just outside the circuit. It soon became clear that I would not be able to land on one-five because I would have to kill myself in order to line up on approach. How about trying it from the other end? I suggested to myself.

The tailwind caught me and I found myself on a right hand downwind for three-three in a shrew's heartbeat. This is better, I thought, nice and clear out here. I was looking south at the time and it did, indeed, look much better. It looked like the daylight it was supposed to be. Then I turned my base leg and...where did that airstrip go? Nothing. Black. I squinted into the light above the mountains and tried to find the airstrip hidden in their shade. It was like staring into a coal-mine.

I began to realize the extent of the crosswind as I crabbed along what should have been the base leg. It's out there some-where, I thought. But where? Slowly my eyes became accustomed to the light and I realized I had not been accounting for the crab angle. I glanced to my right through the passenger window and saw something gray in the black. Long and gray. That's it! I was flying virtually sideways as I aimed for a spot somewhere in the first third of the 2,600-foot gravel runway. Nice and high and hot. All the better to absorb the slip I would need to get lined up in ground effect. I locked onto the far end of the gray blob and set up a five-hundred-foot-per-minute descent rate. I'm landing some-where on this runway, I told myself, my determination constricting my nether-muscles.

Left wing low and rock steady against the gusts, full right rudder, I was a clenched fist as I felt the left gear touch down then the right. Plowing on into the twilight I brought flaps full up to put weight on the wheels and stood on the brakes. What was that noise? It sounded like someone was pounding on the cockpit roof above my head? Thoom-thoom-thoom-thoom! I recognized that sound! It was my heart pounding with adrenaline! Whew!

It was a beautiful landing, with acres of room to spare at the end. And not a soul to witness it except me. But as I taxied into the village and parked the plane, I noticed my soaking armpits might have belied my calm smile to anyone still up at that hour.

"Interesting landing," I stated matter-of-factly to Mary, who was still up at that hour. A bottle of dry red wine, for medicinal purposes only, beckoned from the kitchen counter. After calling in to close my flight plan, I inhaled a glass or two under the scolding glare of my dear wife, who knew all too well what I meant by "interesting".

"You shouldn't be flying at night," she said, flatly.

"It's not night," I answered languidly, as the medicine took effect, "it's 24-hour VFR."

# Chapter Twelve

# The Trench

The last day of the school year was special. Teachers and students shared the relief and the buoyed spirits that accompanied a clean break; a tying off of eight months of work and an end with no strings attached. Come fall, we'd start all over again with a clean slate, crisp new books and the fresh memories of a carefree summer behind us.

With exams finished and marks set, the last day of school became a legal formality more than a day of instruction. As principal of Charles Yohin School, the law required me to open the school for at least one hour, which I did. It had become a tradition to use the short school day to hand out report cards and socialize with the students. They were naturally curious about our plans for the summer.

"You're going to fly to Vancouver?" Lorraine asked.

"That's right. We'll take it in two legs," I answered, pulling down the map of Canada for reference. I pointed to Hudson's Hope, near Fort St. John, British Columbia. "We'll make Hudson's Hope today and stay with some friends. Then we'll take off for Vancouver tomorrow morning and spend some time with my sister before leaving for Toronto." I dragged my yard stick across the map to indicate the route we'd take.

"That's a long way!" Stacey exclaimed, wide-eyed.

Then Walter spoke up. "Didn't you try to fly to Vancouver once before?" he asked, a little note of mischief in his voice.

"Yeah, we sure did," I sighed. The kids knew about our earlier adventure. They were so used to airplanes that they weren't as shocked as southerners tended to be when they heard about our near-death experience at Mackenzie. "The weather's looking really good this time, Walter," I continued, "so don't get your hopes up. I'll be here come fall, you can be sure of that!" The kids all laughed.

I had grown very fond of my students over the past two years. In most ways they were easier to teach and generally nicer and better mannered than the kids I'd taught before. All spoke Slavey fluently in addition to English. They came to school completely bilingual. I encouraged them to use their language in school, and through the Local Education Authority, set up Slavey language classes once a week. I tried to learn the difficult language myself, but never got much farther than "Mahsi cho" (thank you).

Growing up in such an isolated, land-locked settlement had its benefits. For example, the children grew up with an immediate and deep knowledge of nature. They could identify animals by their cries and calls. They could skin a marten, cook bannock and produce intricate bead and quill work, often before they were ten years old. In the time I spent with them, I learned as much from the children as they did from me.

"Remember the earthquake?" Morgan asked, as we chatted informally in the late morning sunlight that streamed through the skylights.

"Yeah, the earthquake! That was scary!" echoed tiny Tina, who was in Kindergarten in the fall of '85 when the earth shook – hard!

"I'll never forget the earthquake, Tina," I answered, flipping through copies of the Nahanni News, the community paper the school produced each week. "Let's see now…here it is!" I retrieved one of our first issues. "Earthquake!" screamed the headline. "6.9 on Richter Scale" followed the sub-heading. Who could forget that?

Who, indeed? Just a few weeks into my first teaching year, a massive earthquake had rocked Mexico City which created an excellent opportunity to introduce the senior students to the subject of plate tectonics, earthquakes and volcanoes.

"Could we ever have an earthquake?" Priscilla had asked, looking worried.

"Not likely," I laughed. "Have the elders ever talked of earthquakes?"

"No," she responded.

"And I doubt you'll ever experience one, either!" I consoled the little group of eager faces. It turned out the lesson included the concept of "irony."

We slept in that Saturday morning, a few weeks later, as was the custom in our household. I arose and headed for the bathroom, hoping to get dibs before Mary or Johnny claimed it. Standing by

118

the sink, I felt a sudden vibration, followed by a rumble beneath the building. At first, I thought the furnace was going to explode. Sometimes it ingested more than the proper amount of fuel before igniting, creating a rumble and "whoosh" not unlike what I was sensing now. Then, suddenly, it felt as though the whole building had been set on uneven rollers and was rumbling, rocking and rolling. A light flashed on in my still-drowsy brain. I shouted to Mary, who was now in the hall, "It's okay! It's only an earthquake!" feeling the latter would be less dangerous than an exploding furnace.

I rushed into the hallway to find Mary and Johnny on the floor on all fours. "Earthquake, Johnny! We're having an earthquake!" Mary shouted excitedly above the din.

The building rocked and swayed as if possessed. The fridge door flew open, spilling its contents across the floor. The fluorescent light fixture cover clattered to the floor. "Wow!" I exclaimed, "This is amazing!" It seemed like minutes but the whole event likely took no more than twenty or thirty seconds. In truth, I loved it. At no time was I really afraid. It was just the most unusual, amazing experience. I rushed to the kitchen window to see how the village had fared.

Outside, the trees were still shaking, hydro lines swaying and odd sounds were emanating from the tank farm, where millions of litres of fuel were sloshing end to end inside the giant tanks. Duffy ran up to our house.

"That was a big one!" he gasped, as he stumbled through the door. "I was working in the new school and I dived out the door headfirst," he reported, "figuring the whole building might fall off the pilings!"

"How big was it? Four or five?" I asked.

"No, that was close to seven!" he replied, still awed by the experience. "I've been through fives and sixes in Alaska and I can tell you this was bigger!"

And so it was. Six point nine and Nahanni sat within a few miles of the epicentre. Fortunately, one-storey log buildings are the perfect structures to withstand earthquakes and no serious damage resulted. The store shelves had been emptied and more light fixtures had broken in the old school. Some cliffs and rocks were rearranged in Nahanni National Park and a few people had taken the earthquake as a sign to stop drinking. Some asked the priest if it was an omen. Father Mary had just cocked one eye and said nothing. Later he confided to me, "One reason is as good as any for some people to stop drinking!" His Parisian accent added a certain humour and poignancy to his unofficial views.

"That was the scariest thing I've ever experienced," Priscilla said, as I ushered the students out of the building into the warm June day and I prepared to officially put a period on the end of the school year, 1986-'87.

"Well, I'll never say 'never' again," I replied, "but I don't think you have to worry about another one for a few hundred years. Now you kids have a good and safe summer."

With that, I locked up the school and headed for Papa X-Ray, parked next to the nursing station across from the store. Mary already had it loaded and Johnny was eager to go. "When are we leaving, Dad?"

We blasted off the strip a half-hour later, bound for Vancouver, the newly overhauled engine sucking us up into a perfect sky above the muskeg and forest below. A quick bathroom stop and a topping off of the tanks held us up less than a half-hour at Fort Nelson. Soon we were cruising at 3,500 feet along the eastern edge of the mountains, southbound for our first overnight stop, Hudson's Hope, B.C.

An old high school acquaintance, now principal of the local high school in Hudson's Hope, offered his hospitality and two warm beds for the night. To my delight, and the knowing fateful nods of all others present, Barry turned out to be a pilot as well. His 1961 172 rested at the gorgeous 5,200-foot asphalt strip built during the construction of the Bennet Dam, nearby. After an evening spent twisting the stories of our lives into tales of monumental courage and accomplishment over a bottle of scotch, we found ourselves leaning over a VFR chart spread on UPX's cowl the next morning.

"It's a piece of cake," Barry said. "As soon as you get air underneath you, head for this big peak. Then, just hang a left and boom, you're in Prince George." He punctuated his advice with a poke at the chart and a point toward the mountainous horizon to the southwest.

"Great!" I responded, leaning over the chart, felt marker poised. "I'll just get a heading off the chart and we're outta here. I can file in the air." Let's see, I thought, we add the deviation, or do we subtract?...hmmm. There, that's got it. I wasn't too concerned. It was a beautiful day and the landmarks were unmistakable — lakes, mountains and rivers. It really would be a cakewalk.

We climbed in. "Everybody take their Gravol?" I asked, getting nods in return. I didn't want any barfing to detract from what I knew was going to be one of the best flights ever. The Gravol was already taking its toll on three-year-old Johnny, who was starting to nod off in the back seat as I lined up on two-three and fire-walled the throttle. The new engine roared as we galloped down the pavement and floated off, waggling our wings to Barry, waving below.

I banked to my hastily-determined heading and settled back to enjoy the view as we climbed under full power. The little engine clawed the air toward our planned altitude, 8,500 feet, nose-bleed territory in a 145-horse Cessna 172. The breathtaking view enveloped us as we left the picturesque little town behind. Ahead, perfect VFR. Ahhh. Bliss. Then...

"It doesn't seem right to me," Mary mused aloud, more mystified than concerned.

"What doesn't seem right?" I asked, hesitantly, with the caution I had long since learned to apply to airborne discussions with my wife, The Navigator. Mary was justifiably cautious when commenting about aviation matters. Most men are biologically incapable of accepting their wife's advice when it comes to navigating, on the ground or in the air. Wives unfairly apply logic and good sense in attempting to prove our inherently good judgment wrong. To make matters worse, they tend to be right more often than not. At least, my wife was.

"That lake over there," she answered thoughtfully, pointing dead ahead without looking up from the chart that she was studying intently. "We shouldn't be heading toward it, we should be parallel to it, according to this pink line you drew on the chart."

Picky, picky, I thought, as I scanned the awesome panorama ahead and below. Twelve-thousand-foot peaks rose up around us, twice the height of the mountains of the Nahanni, high enough to make a wife nervous, for some reason. I checked the chart and the situation ahead.

Clearly, someone had moved the lake. Either that or my heading was wrong. What if I had calculated the deviation wrong? I did some quick mental arithmetic and then I felt it, The Blush. Better not admit such stupidity too early in this trip, I thought, as I realized that I had, indeed, plotted a course 60 degrees north of where it ought to have been. Better think quick. Don't want to jeopardize the confidence of the crew.

"Let's just head across here to the valley, now that we're going this way, anyway," I offered, weakly.

"You mean we are going the wrong way?" In those few words Mary managed to convey her perspective on aviation in general: we were in an aluminum Volkswagen hanging from one tiny propeller thousands of feet above certain death and the trained pilot of this aircraft is casually going the wrong way through the Rocky Mountains!

Okay, I thought, I guess the confidence is jeopardized. It's salvage time. "Well," I began, as confidently as the situation allowed, "if you look over to that mountain we were just talking about, you can see there's a rain shower nearby." Which was, in fact, true. A small black cloud did indeed block the proper, more direct route, although it was quite small, actually. "Now, why mess with it when we can just fly straight ahead, catch the valley and follow it south to Prince George?" I concluded. I had to keep any shred of confidence alive here. After all, I was the one who convinced her of the practicality of the upcoming adventure. We would fly all the way to Vancouver, I had argued, and it would be easy and beautiful. The mountains...the rivers...

"There's the lake," Mary pointed to the right and down to our next landmark, the north fork of Williston Lake that appeared as we cleared the ridge and banked left, down the trench. "Whooo!" she shuddered, "I'll never forget that trip to Mackenzie. I like that lake a lot better from up here." I knew she'd dig that story up, but I plunged on, hopefully.

"See, that shower looks pretty dark over there. It's a good thing we came this way."

"Yes, dear," she conceded. She knew. They always know. This had better be an uneventful day or the Vancouver to Toronto trip coming up next week was in real trouble. In the meantime, I'd better grease this on at Prince George and be Mr. Nice Guy for at least an hour.

Topped tanks, emptied bladders, a quick sandwich and Prince George disappeared behind us. I took Papa X-Ray and its somewhat mollified crew up to 6,500 feet for the fun part of the trip. We could clear the ridge nicely and then descend into the Trench slowly, losing altitude with the river, down toward Hope and beyond.

We weren't in the official "Trench", not the one most pilots up here refer to as the Trench. But, a trench is a trench as long as its bounded on both sides by mountains and the trip to Prince

George and Williams Lake fit that description accurately. Beyond Billy's Puddle, however, we headed southwest, toward...quiet now, The Fraser Canyon. Why the big fuss? It was just another stretch of forbidding terrain with no possibility of a successful forced landing, right? We'd been flying such country constantly since I got my licence last summer, right? Right?

"Oh, my God, The Fraser Canyon," she whispered through the intercom. That's why I'd had it installed, I thought, just to hear remarks like that.

We cleared a rounded peak at 6,500 feet and banked south. Just another canyon, I thought, cracking the throttle open another notch. They said to fly the new engine hard, didn't they, 2500 rpm or better, they said, when you're breaking these engines in. No problem. One of the few treats of major overhauls is that you get to fly flat-out with a clear conscience. Gas consumption, dear? Sorry, nothing I can do about it, gotta fly her hard. I gotta protect the investment, right?

Hmmm. I studied the sky ahead and noted the blue sky seemed to meet some distinct gray up there a piece. Yup, there appears to be a ceiling farther on down. Better get a little lower. Is that a headwind I'm feeling?

"Dad! Stop that!" My son was conscious and critical of my aviating. Whummmpp, another blast hit us like an invisible fist. I glanced over at Mary. Now why would I do that? What would I expect to see, a beaming, confident wife, with a "you can do it" look on her face? Unlikely. Terror, that's what I saw and her emotions were quickly filling the little 172's cabin. Bamm! That was a bad one. Well, it was only to be expected. We had picked up a stiff headwind which, when funneled up the canyon, took the rather rough shapes of the cliffs and terrain around us. In short, we were getting hammered.

"It's all right son," I soothed through the intercom to the young lad. "It's just like bumps on the road; a little rough, but they won't hurt us." Why had I put a four-place intercom in this plane? I wondered.

"What?" Mary asked. Oops, guess I said that out loud.

"Nothing, dear. Um, I'm glad I put that intercom in the plane." She gave me a quizzical look and glanced back nervously at our bundle of flesh and blood in the back seat. I followed her gaze. The little tike looked like a Bighorn sheep with that big Telex headset squeezing his baby face.

123

As I fought with the controls, I took stock of our position. Why not descend as we head down the valley, I had reasoned. No need to be up in the stratosphere. As a result of that remarkable deduction, we were now down to 2,500 feet and heading for a narrow pass in the canyon. The wind, roaring up the valley at thirty knots, tried to squeeze through the opening toward us. It was a natural venturi tube. As we approached the pass, I noticed our ground speed dropping until we appeared almost motionless. There was no question, the caboose on that freight winding its way through the tunnels below was gaining on us. Okay, we weren't exactly motionless, there was plenty of motion of the up, down and sideways variety. We weren't going anywhere fast, though, so I had lots of time to consider the lowering ceiling ahead.

I cut a corner over a spectacular forested peak to eliminate one tight turn and pointed UPX down the darkening valley ahead. The radio crackled.

"Alpha Bravo Charlie, we copy, out." I heard the last bit on frequency 126.7 and saw what looked like a Seneca well above us and heading downstream. Now what was all that good altitude doing above us when we were getting hammered down here? I began to think my wife's assessment of my skills was closer to reality than my own.

"Alpha Bravo Charlie, Uniform Papa X-Ray is a 172 below and behind you. What's the weather like up there?"

"UPX, ABC, not bad up here at all. Looks like it's lowering though. 'Course, we're IFR..." He let that hang in the air as if to say that anybody who flies in this kind of stuff should be IFR. Well, of course they were IFR! No need to brag about it!

Okay, there was room above and I'd had enough of this pounding. I hauled the plane up into a climb and noticed the turbulence ease almost immediately. This meant that I had put my trusting family through the preceding terror for nothing. That's okay, I reasoned, they'll be in the proper frame of mind for what's ahead.

It wasn't particularly rough when we were forced back down to 2,500 feet by the ceiling a half-hour later but I was beginning to develop yet more respect for the mountains. At least before I was down here because I chose to be down here. Now I had to be down here and I didn't like it. Then it started to rain.

Six miles, five miles, four miles, I had decided that when it got to three miles visibility I would turn around. The back door was open. Hope was ahead — not the emotion, but the town, the town of Hope and, yes, there it was! All we had to do was get around the corner at Hope and it was flatland the rest of the way. Flatland, indeed. Flat, gray and three miles in rain. And, wait, I don't remember there being these mountains stuck in the middle of this "flat" land. Enough. Time to throw in the towel. I flipped open the Flight Supplement to the very first page of listed airports and dialed 119.4

"Abbotsford Tower, Uniform Papa X-Ray."

"Uniform Papa X-Ray, Abbotsford Tower, go ahead."

"Abbotsford Tower, Uniform Papa X-Ray ten to fifteen miles east at fifteen hundred feet VFR out of Williams Lake, destination Abbotsford, with the information squawking twelve hundred, request DF steer." There I'd said it. After the mismanaged navigation, the turbulence and now the rapidly diminishing visibility, I was not about to end the day splattered against some rock in the lower mainland. Mary wouldn't like that. So I let the tower lead me in on a leash like a bad puppy.

"Uniform Papa X-Ray, Abbotsford, steer two five five degrees." I complied and glued my eyes to the panel. Being led in like a forlorn dog was not the way I had planned to end the day, but I knew of other pilots who had fared much worse. After all, we had logged another Great Flying Experience. We had now flown The Trench. Right, Mary?

"That's right, dear."

"Are we there yet, Dad?"

# Chapter Thirteen

# Over the rocks

"No big deal," the elderly gent assured me as we browsed through publications in the aviator shop in downtown Vancouver. "I've flown Vancouver to Calgary many times in my 172. You could do the whole trip at 5,500 feet, if you wanted to." Of course, I didn't need reassurance. Not much, anyway. It was my wife who exhibited pre-flight trepidation at the upcoming flight across the rocks. But much of her confidence, or lack of it, stemmed from my confidence, or lack of it.

"Which route do you take?" I probed further.

"If you've got the ceiling, just get right up there and take it as directly as you can. At 9,500 you'll easily cut most of the big corners and save all kinds of fuel." The good, solid anecdotal opinions of members of the flying fraternity served to fill and smooth any cracks in my own resolve. I was ready.

All we needed now was good weather, anything but the drizzle and ragged ceiling that had welcomed us a few days earlier. Much has been written about the eroding effects of rain on the unstable, muddy cliffs that flanked British Columbia highways. Somewhat less was recorded about its effects in eroding confidence in "my husband the pilot". Family fan flights around Abbotsford did little to recoup my flagging image.

First up, Barry Games, my strapping, tall, cockney brother-in-law. "We're not moving!" he exclaimed five minutes into his first ever flight in a "tiny" airplane. Here it was, 1987, and Barry had never been in an airplane smaller than the Boeing 707 that had brought him to the colony from his native England years back.

"Hundred and ten miles per hour," I shot back, defensively, pointing at the airspeed indicator. But logic and established aerodynamic theory impressed Bear not a jot. Nor was he looking where I was pointing. He was looking down and gripping the hand-hold above his seat as though it were a ledge fifty stories above a city street. His calm exterior masked hidden terror.

"I feel as though I'm sitting on a kitchen chair on top of a nine-hundred-foot tall flagpole," he said, laughing a nervous laugh.

"Uh, okaaaay," I conceded in defeat. "Let's head her back in." I had long since learned to avoid converting the acrophobic in mid-flight, if ever. Wobbling on rubber knees, Barry navigated toward the car after the ten-minute adventure. My sister Carol was less fearful but has not asked for a repeat experience over the years. Perhaps Mary, my somewhat maligned mate, absorbed more of my scorn than she deserved, I thought. Who wouldn't be a little nervous about flying over the mountains to Calgary in a 172, newly-rebuilt engine notwithstanding?

Old friends, Richard Baker and Lynne Howes, enjoyed the afternoon cruise over the lower mainland and expressed their heartfelt thanks for the opportunity. There. I felt better. Now, to a quiet evening and a good night's rest. Tomorrow we fly the rocks.

"Oh God of the monocoque airframe, Gods of Bernoulli and Continental," I whispered quietly, eyes closed, moments after awakening the next morning. My sleeping wife was oblivious to my prayer, so I continued. "Please, oh, please make a miracle. In this land of liquid sunshine, waterlogged citizenry and ceilings indefinite, make me some flying weather. Banish scud and one-mile visibility, soothe and calm the turbulent ether, although a gentle westerly would not be unwelcome."

I opened my eyes. The thin window curtains glowed an unearthly amber. Heart pounding, I crept close, sensing my prayers were to be answered. A pale, unfamiliar yellow disc appeared low on the horizon, no doubt startling any early-rising delta dwellers. Trembling hands pulled back the cloth veil and...deliverance! Above and around for as far as my squinting eyes could see, a great blue ocean of sky appeared. And there, floating in it, a blazing sun, gloating in its celestial solitude. Quickly I calmed myself, knowing all too well that this rare Vancouver sky represented but a tiny portion of our planned flight path.

"Looks pretty good," I muttered casually to Mary, now stirring under the sheets, as I threw on my clothes and made for the phone to get the official weather. Mary's face reflected that momentary paradox I'd learned to recognize as delight/fear. Delight because the weather was good and we were going and fear because we were going.

127

"Can't you do something about this pesky blue sky?" I joked to the briefer on the other end of the line. "It's liable to frighten Vancouverites back into their mossy dwellings."

"What you see is what you get," the disembodied voice chuckled into my happy ear. "'course, you will have about a ten-knot tailwind to contend with, but you're clear all the way to Calgary and then some."

This is why we fly, I thought, as Papa X-Ray lugged our little family slowly up to my planned 9,500-foot cruising altitude. Below us, the brilliant Irish-green patchwork quilt of the Fraser Delta. To the south, Mount Baker rose like Fujiyama with thousands of feet of clear blue air above its towering summit. To the north and east, smaller forest-carpeted mountains, sparkling blue rivers and lakes at their feet, spread ever wider on the horizon as we rose to equal and then climb above their height.

This is why we fly, this is why we endure the quizzical glances of the earth-bound skeptics. This is why we pour money into the money-pit of general aviation, why we lure and cajole our friends and families into joining us in the sky. Who could not love flying, when flying is like this?

I pulled my eyes from the natural wonders below and ahead and glanced at Johnny, nose pressed against the Plexiglas, as wide-eyed as his proud dad. His Transformers lay abandoned on the seat beside him unable to compete with the pure splendor of the scene unfolding outside. A rare moment, indeed, when we could all enjoy the wonder of powered flight; me, my son and my mate.

"How high are you planning to go?" she asked casually, her eyes scouring the charts on her knees. The tone was not wife-like; it was the objective voice of The Navigator. She glanced up to survey the peaks ahead, then down again to the charts.

"Ninety-five hundred," I answered. My exhilaration crested and began to wane as I realized that, for Mary, happiness was still inextricably bonded to good navigation no matter how glorious the weather.

"Some of these peaks are a lot higher than that," she stated flatly. "We'll have to go around them, of course."

"Of course, dear," I replied, just a trace of arrogance creeping into my voice. Did she think I would try to fly through them? I calmed myself. "We'll fly the valleys and highways but, at this height, we'll be able to cut a few corners..." I let that hang in the air.

The little mountain-hedged town disappeared behind our left wing and from then on, as the saying goes, we were beyond Hope. As I examined our path ahead, I could feel Mary's direct glare warming the right side of my face.

"What do you mean, cut corners?" she leveled at me, her tone implying minimal discussion would be tolerated.

"Well, like this," I said, starting a gentle right-hand bank. I eased myself into the topic as the highway below made a wide arc around a mountain, only to appear again below and ahead. "We can cut across here, see, instead of following the road inch by inch." Mary examined the route ahead, checked and double-checked her chart and began to visibly relax a little as she realized we would clear the peak by more than three thousand feet.

"Just as long as we stay on course."

"No problem. We can practically see all the way to Calgary..." I started, then thought better of it. This was no time to make ill-considered predictions.

"Remember Prince George?"

Oh, unkind cut! How could she? Go ahead, I thought, drag that one out. So I had taken the wrong heading out of Hudson's Hope for Prince George last week. So she found and corrected the error! I knew. She knew. I knew that she knew that I knew. That she would mention it now was a clear drawing of the line. Cross it, she was saying, and matrimonial horrors beyond your comprehension would befall you. I said nothing.

Once again the Gravol had rendered Johnny unconscious. Sleeping peacefully in the back seat, a Transformer cradled in his lap, he was missing most of the trip. But, as I'd said many times, I'd rather have a sleeping passenger than a puking passenger. It was too bad that Gravol calmed the mind as it calmed the stomach. It was the price you paid. Frankly, I think it had a calming effect on Mary, who had been known to doze a little herself, although her finger tended to stay glued to the highlighted course on the map in her lap as she slept.

"Fly her hard," they had said at the overhaul shop, when I had called them a month back. And so I did. At almost 2400 rpm the little O-300 was turning out as much power as she could at this altitude, and with the tailwind we were making short work of this trip. A little more than an hour from takeoff we started our descent into Kelowna, where I had planned a fuel stop. As our ears began to pop, I wondered whether the fuel we would burn getting back up to cruise after our stop might not equal or better what we would save by getting fuel here in the first place. A smarter pilot would know for sure, one with more facility on the "whiz-wheel." I preferred to let full fuel tanks take sway over mathematical calculations. There was no arguing with a full tank of fuel.

"Why are we stopping here?" Mary asked, casually.

"Fuel," I answered. And that was that. At least there was one part of aviation that went unchallenged in this cockpit.

Kelowna was home to the shop that overhauled the O-300, so while UPX got her tanks topped with 80/87, I jogged over to Okanagan Aero Engine and chatted for a few minutes. I hoped they would tell me again that I should fly her hard.

"Fly her hard," they said.

Even at full throttle it's a long way up to 9,500 feet in a 172. The ear-popping kept Johnny awake and I was glad of it, as the scenery of the interior matched the magnificence of the coastal range. We cut corners safely here and there until the Rockies loomed ahead. We rounded one craggy rock face, then another, snow still hiding in crevices and on summits even now in late June.

"Here, take it for a minute so I can shoot a couple of pictures," I said, taking my hands off the controls and reaching for the camera. You had to be firm and quick about this, I had learned. Any discussion would result in a missed shot and an uptight wife.

"Oh, no," Mary whimpered, tentatively taking the yoke. "Oh, please, Jim, I hate this." I knew she hated it. I also knew she could do it, although it took a little nudge. Then there's the revenge factor. You wanna be critical of my aviating, well, how about flying a nautical mile in my shoes, eh?

"Arghhhhhhh!" she cried, not too loudly but with enough fervor for me to glance away from my viewfinder in time to see us leaning into a medium right-hand turn, my wife wide-eyed, both hands frozen to the control column.

"Just turn it back to the left, like a car," I lectured, a bit impatiently. Grabbing the yoke abruptly, I jerked the aircraft to a level attitude. Maybe now she'd have a bit more respect for my flying skills, I thought.

"Arghhhhhhh!" We were now in a left-hand turn. No matter, I had taken the shots. My skills as a pilot were now reaffirmed. I took the controls in time to cut a large chunk off the corner at Roger's Pass with no argument from my now subdued "copilot." A wide valley opened below us and that fat and happy feeling began to rise when...

"I have to go pee."

"What?"

"I have to go pee!" Johnny said, louder this time. Mary looked out the window at the craggy peaks just beyond the wing, then at me and then at Johnny. Well, that's why we carry his potty, we both thought simultaneously. Never thought of actually using it, mind you. The calm air was a big help and in no time I heard the telltale tinkle from the back seat. I began to squirm. There was something about running water...I looked at Mary to see her looking back at me.

"You too, huh?" I asked, hoping for a negative indication. She nodded.

"Me too," I admitted, knowing there was no place to land.

There is no dignified way to relieve yourself in the cabin of a 172 at 9,500 feet, especially if you are of female design. Suffice to say that I was glad we were a family unit not unaccustomed to sharing such intimacies in emergencies. For the unconvinced, I offer this simple fact: it can be done. We did it and we felt much better about the remainder of the trip as a result.

Our bladders relieved, we were in a better frame of mind to enjoy Lake Louise, passing off our right wing, a glittering emerald in a diamond setting. It was followed by Banff, a few minutes later, just around the bend. Too soon we were propelled out of the last valley into the foothills by a more aggressive tailwind than the one that had launched us at Abbotsford, less than four hours earlier. We had planned to make Red Deer, Alberta, our final destination that day which meant a fuel stop at Springbank near Calgary.

"Top her off?" the young fellow asked as I stepped out at the pumps.

"Um. Let me see, no, just fill the left tank," I answered, surprising myself a little. Perhaps it was luck. I wasn't thinking about our departure but I should have been. At three thousand nine hundred and thirty-seven feet above sea level, Springbank was a caution on any day. On a hot day, such as the day now unfolding, most planes needed the full 3,400 feet of Runway two-five/zero-seven. Today the wind was blowing just a tad northerly and Runway three-four was active, all three thousand hot asphalt feet of it.

About two thousand of those feet were now behind Papa X-Ray, as I tugged at the yoke, searching for an indication that UPX wanted to fly again today. I became increasingly grateful for my casual decision to forego a full fuel load and with no more than five hundred feet of runway ahead the little 172 was flying. Or was it? A bead of sweat formed between my eyes, slid down my nose and dropped on my lower lip, which was moving now, encouraging Papa X-Ray to fly. Like now! The little O-300 gasped in the thin, hot air and every available molecule of the same thin air was struggling to lift that big wing. We cleared a barbed-wire fence off the end of the runway by no more than thirty feet. The pucker factor was a 7/10.

"Was that close?" Mary asked, almost casually.

How do you answer that question? I wondered. "Normal for these parts," I breathed, willing UPX up another hundred feet and pointing her nose toward Red Deer.

Density altitude is more than a measure of aircraft performance. It is a measure of the density of the pilot, too. After all, it would have cheered our grieving relatives not a whit to know that we had survived the rockiest stretch of air in North America only to be dragged to our doom by a four-foot-high barbed-wire fence; the highest object within ten miles on the bald prairie just west of Calgary, east of the rocks.

# Chapter Fourteen

# Last legs

"Winds zero five zero at five gusting ten. Uniform Papa X-Ray is cleared to land zero-seven," Thunder Bay control tower welcomed us on 118.1.

"Papa X-Ray, check remarks, cleared to land," I acknowledged. We were still miles back, not too far from Kakabeka Falls, but traffic was light as I set up for a long final leg to the runway. The Rockies, the prairies and the limitless lake land of Kenora were behind us and we had two planned legs to go. It wasn't late but we were tired, having flown all the way from Dauphin, Manitoba where we'd visited with brother Lin for an evening. We decided to call it a day and overnight at the Valhalla Inn just off the end of the runway at Thunder Bay.

The next morning we began to regret that we hadn't taken advantage of the good weather the day before. Johnny and Mary splashed in the hotel pool while I made hourly calls to Flight Service.

"Naw. It's still blocked practically all the way," the specialist advised over and over. A persistent scud blanketed the north shore of Lake Superior from Thunder Bay to Wawa. Johnny was having a good time for the second day at the Valhalla but the Brampton Flying Club awaited me to the east, on the far side of that pesky blanket of cloud. I wanted to get my night endorsement and I needed to get started. Enough of this northern Ontario weather, already!

I decided to take the shuttle van over to the Flight Service Station just in case my presence would make a difference to the weather. I killed time in the airport, dropping in every hour for the latest weather. They were about to start charging me rent when the briefer spoke up. "Since the northern route is blocked, why don't you go the American route, along the south shore of Superior. People do it all the time."

Why not, indeed? I thought, checking the chart. The shortest way south was...to cut across the lake.

I called Mary and instructed her to pack up, pay the bill and come over. Later, as I dropped the chart in her lap and taxied for two-five, she began to absorb the reason why we could now suddenly fly even though the weather hadn't changed. My wife, The Navigator, scanned the chart intently and intoned, "But, but that's...over water!"

"We'll be at 9,500 feet," I responded carefully, "so we'll be able to glide to within inches of land from the mid-point and besides, we'll be locked onto radar the whole way. Why, if we should so much as hiccup, Search and Rescue would be down there to meet us by the time we touched the water." Why did that not sound as reassuring as it should have? Then the clincher, "Other people do it all the time."

Her silent, blank stare shouted, "So what?" We took off, climbing out past the island called the Sleeping Giant and reached cruise altitude ten miles over Lake Superior's forbidding expanse. I loved this. It was a whole new experience. Hmmm. What was that?

"What was what?" Mary answered, startled by my urgent tone. Had I said that out loud? I was sure I had just thought it.

"Nothing, nothing. Not to worry," I answered, a little unnerved by my verbal slip and by that new sound the engine was starting to make. A quick glance across the instruments revealed needles pointing steadily where they were supposed to be pointing, especially the altimeter, showing 9,500 feet. I glanced back over my shoulder, past our sleeping child to see Isle Royal far below and behind and then spun around to scan ahead to the vague outline of the distant American shore, a peninsula jutting out into Lake Superior. Below, the cold, deep water, fifty miles of it in total, waited like a giant blue hand, ready to catch us should we fall. Then, that sound again!

I had heard of "over-water rough". Aircraft mechanics joked about it all the time. It was the sound a pilot heard from a perfectly-tuned, harmonically-balanced aircraft engine flying over a large body of water. Uncanny how real it sounds, I thought. Although I knew that if the engine really did miss, really did cough, I'd know it immediately, for it had happened on two memorable occasions. A fouled plug was the culprit in both cases. When the gases in the offending cylinder failed to ignite as I locked onto my final approach at Dauphin a few days ago, I knew it all right. The unmistakable sound was delivered to my cerebral cortex by a charge of adrenaline that left me shaking for an hour after landing. No, this was "over-water rough," all right or I'd know otherwise.

Resigned to her fate, Mary pressed her finger to the orange line tracing our passage over the blue route below us and cast her stolid gaze toward the southern horizon. "Land!" she shouted. Excitement and relief emanated from the right seat as the tiny peninsula appeared on the watery horizon ahead.

"Houghton tower," I started my transmission, "Uniform Papa X-Ray, over…"

"This is HOE-TON, not HOW-TON, tower, Canadian Uniform X-Ray Papa, go ahead."

Is this what flying the in the United States is going to be like? I wondered. Are they going to correct my British-based, Canadian usage of the language we helped invent? And are they going to scramble my registration every time?

"HOE-ton tower, Uniform *Papa* X-Ray, twenty north at niner point five, VFR out of Thunder Bay, destination Canadian Sault, squawking twelve hundred, position report, over."

"Uniform X-Ray Papa," he tried again, "Houghton tower, radar identified."

And that was that. We locked onto the south shore string of VORs and beelined straight to Sault Ste. Marie. Even Mary became a convert to our new route. We were to fly the American skies many times after this initiation and the Americans would tend to scramble our Canadian registrations regularly; not surprising since their own registrations consisted of an "N" followed by mere bland numbers. That said, there were no friendlier nor more accommodating folks than the aviation community to the south. It was always a pleasure to visit their welcoming skies and magnificent airports.

"I have to pee, Dad!" Johnny was almost jumping up and down back there. Bladder pressure was critical on three fronts and nerves and hunger were close to meltdown when we landed safely in Sault Ste. Marie. We called it a day and repaired to the nearest motel where we tucked into their Wednesday Special, an all-you-can-eat pickerel dinner, accompanied by all-you-can-drink beer. Johnny drank the coffee creamers.

We awoke the next morning under a wall-to-wall blue hemisphere of clear. Not a hint of last night's pickerel and beer clouded my head as I sidled up to the pay phones at the motel to call FSS and get the official word on the weather. A lanky fellow was draped over the pay phone next to me, receiver pressed to his ear.

"Wasn't that weather a corker yesterday?" Eye contact said he was talking to me and not to the phone. The Flight Supplement balanced on top of the phone said he was a pilot.

"We took the south shore and the weather was great," I answered him casually.

"Geez, not me!" he said. "I came in past Wawa and was in and out of the crud all the way here!"

"You flew in by the northern route, yesterday?" I asked, not believing anyone would have tried that. Who was this guy?

"Yes, sir, it was close. Couldn't see the front of the engine cowling. Had to have the tower here give me a DF steer!" he went on, a swagger in his voice.

"That's why we went south," I returned. "Didn't you get a briefing in Thunder Bay?"

"Oh, hell yes, I did. But I thought, by God, I've always wanted to fly east, just once in my life and no by-God-weather is going to stop me!"

Once in your life is right! I thought. Did they really make pilots like this? I was beginning to feel more superior than ever.

"So you've never been this route before?" I was asking for it.

"Nope. In fact, I just got my ticket back after ten years. Quadruple by-pass. Haven't flown since '77. I put this 172 together myself. Slapped a hundred-and-eighty-horse Lycoming in it and blasted off. Got a good deal on that plane, too. She was all bent up from a bad landing so I got her cheap and, well, here I am!"

And no one more amazed than me, I thought.

"So, you've done the trip before, eh? Why don't we fly the rest of the way together? I just love that kind of flying!" he enthused.

I hate that kind of flying, I thought. I get a sore neck looking out for the other plane and it scares the bejeezuz out of me. "One-eighty Lycoming, eh? Your plane is a lot faster than mine. I'd just slow you down," I replied, weakly.

"No problem. I can fly her slow or fast, don't matter to me!" He could not be discouraged, it seemed. Well, maybe if I dragged my feet he'd get ahead of us and leave us alone.

"I guess it can't hurt," I lied. I took my time on my pre-flight check hoping he'd get off first and fly head of us. As we launched to the south, I listened for his transmissions but heard none. I began to relax and enjoy the view.

"There he is!" yelled Mary an hour later as we approached Manitoulin Island. "He's coming up on our right side!" I strained to look out her side and there he was, filling the whole window, blasting up and past us, grinning and waving as he went.

"Don't let that maniac out of your sight," I ordered, knowing she was as interested in living as I was. I raised the elderly cowboy on the radio. "You've got the bigger engine," I suggested gamely. "Why don't you go on ahead?"

"Roger dodger, pal! Say, where's the next stop?"

"Just check your chart. We'll pass Tobermory and then head on down the Bruce Peninsula to Wiarton for fuel," I responded.

"Don't have a chart for these parts. Got one for Toronto, though." I couldn't believe my ears.

"It's the same chart," I radioed back, hoping somebody else was listening to this nonsense in case I ever had to defend myself in court. "Just flip it over and you'll see the northern part."

"Ah, hell, buddy, I'm too busy taking pictures to read a chart. I'll just follow you."

The Manitoulin to Wiarton leg was one of the most beautiful rides of the whole trip. We had looked forward to a leisurely scenic flight over the aquamarine water and picture postcard islands but today no one in our plane was looking down. Even Johnny got into the game.

"There he is Dad!" he called from the back seat. Since the modified Skyhawk practically filled the windshield, this announcement was not a big help, although it was nice to see Johnny taking some interest in aviation at last.

"Thanks, son. I've got him." All eyes were locked onto the tail of the modified 172 now disappearing ahead and below to our great relief. We crossed the water and were passing Tobermory when Mary pointed down and to the right.

"There he is again!" she yelled. Blasting up toward us, the cowboy roared past as the radio crackled to life.

"Thought that was Wiarton," he laughed, "almost put her down before I realized it!"

"Nope, that's Tobermory, all right," I said, wondering what was next. "Tune your VOR to Wiarton and follow it in. You can call them on 122.2."

"Never use those VORs," he responded. "122.2 you say? Okay! See you there!" And he was gone. As our wheels touched down at Wiarton, we were mildly surprised to see the terror of the skies safely parked at the pumps. I taxied up and got out, resigned to my fate.

"Just about missed her," he started, "but I got here, right?"

"You sure did," I said, wanting to change the subject. "How do you like that extra horsepower? Must take a lot of rudder on climb-out to keep her straight."

"Hell, I never bother with rudder! If she wants to fly side-ways, that's okay with me! To be perfectly honest, I suppose the government people wouldn't care for my paperwork on this baby. But, hell, it gets me where I'm going, don't it?"

As the cowboy headed for the washrooms, I suggested that we take off first and if he needed any help navigating he could catch up with us later. "We'll monitor 122.2 so we'll know when you're off and then listen for you on 122.9," I said, as we headed for our plane. "Let's go!" I said to Mary. "Maybe we can get far enough ahead and lose this maniac."

Ten minutes out of Wiarton we were still listening, waiting for him to announce his departure but the airwaves were quiet. But not the air itself.

"There he is!" yelled Mary. "Right off our wing!" And there he was indeed. Apparently he viewed radio work with the same disdain he applied to every other aspect of aviation regulations. I switched to 122.9.

"Didn't hear you leave," I started. "Just where are you head-ing, exactly?"

"Burlington!"

Burlington! This guy was going down to thread the needle between a half-dozen airports, including Toronto's Pearson Inter-national, and he couldn't tell Tobermory from Wiarton.

"Check the chart, Mary," I said, "get him a clear route to Bur-lington and may the aviation community forgive us." I keyed the mike. "We're coming up to a highway that takes you straight down to Burlington," I radioed. "Not this first one here, mind you, the next one." He roared ahead and banked sharply right, heading down the wrong road.

"Not that one," I repeated, "come back! It's the next major highway!"

We watched him bank left and pull alongside. His wings be-gan to waggle. For a moment I thought he was waving goodbye. Then I saw both his hands in the window, holding a camera.

"Got a good shot there! I'll send you a print. Thanks for everything." And he was gone, down the right highway, for what that was worth.

In a little while the familiar Caledon Hills appeared below and the friendly orange rooftops of the Brampton Flying Club beyond. It was good to be back. I hoped my old instructor, Doug Hannah, would be available to teach me my night work. I thought about Doug and his demanding instructions, especially cross-country navigation, and wondered what he'd say about the cowboy, now down in the thick of it somewhere to the southwest.

"Do you think he made it?" Mary asked, as we touched down on Brampton's Runway one-five.

"I don't know, but let's monitor the local news broadcasts tonight, just in case."

"We're here! We're here!" Johnny chanted, then he broke into song. "You are my sunshine..."

"My only sunshine," Mary and I joined in with his favourite song. We were still singing when we stepped out onto the friendly tarmac of BFC.

"People will think we're nuts!" Mary laughed.

"Think, nothing," I answered. "These people already know us." We all laughed and looked where Johnny was pointing and waving. It was Olive, standing by the good old gold Dodge, smiling and waving. Right on time.

# Chapter Fifteen

# Fly by night

"Still in one piece, I see," Doug Hannah said, extending a hand. His sense of humour was still intact a year after he had shepherded me through my frantic private pilot's course.

"Still have your doubts?" I countered, returning the good-natured banter that had characterized dozens of hours together in Papa X-Ray the previous summer.

Doug was his usual dapper self, grinning his "here we go again" grin as we worked out an instruction schedule that would culminate in adding a night endorsement to my "single-engine land" ticket. But there was no rush this time. I needed only ten hours of instrument and night work to complete the course and I had all of July and most of August to do it.

"Well, let's see how much you forgot," he sighed, as he reached for a hood and made for the door. "Nothing more dangerous than a hundred-hour pilot, especially one who's been flying the bush for a year."

"Two hundred," I corrected as I followed him to the plane. I was determined to show him what an ace I'd become.

"Ah, yes, Papa X-Ray," Doug mused as we taxied for one-five. "It still has the barrel DG, I see," he went on, mumbling to himself, "and the old 300 radio. You know, this is 1987 not 1887, Jim."

He dialed up 123.4 on the black, dented relic, called for a radio check and feigned surprised when the cheery voice came back, "Papa X-Ray, read you five by five."

Doug turned his attention to the equally suspicious ADF. "And this old thing...yup, same ol' UPX."

"But the engine's been overhauled," I shot back.

"But it's still an O-300," he sighed, knowing I liked my O-300 in spite of the usual good arguments against it. It was underpowered, expensive to overhaul and notorious for carburetor icing but it was the engine that powered UPX, the first and only airplane I ever loved. I liked it and was about to tell him so when he handed me the hood.

"Here, put this on," he started, "and see how straight you can keep it on the takeoff roll with that barrel DG you seem to like so much."

I had never worn a hood before. There had been no requirement for hood work for my private ticket the previous year. I thought he'd at least let me take off before putting me to work but Doug was Doug. He liked to make things interesting. For example, a year ago we had been doing air work at 4,000 feet when he'd instructed me to put down some flap and do a slip. Aha! I thought, this is a trick! This plane is placarded against slips with flaps extended. "I cannot comply," I'd replied.

"No, really, let's try a slip with the flaps extended," he had pressed, getting a little irritated.

"No way, man," I'd replied, "I'm not going to fall for that one. If I do it you'll dump on me about flying illegal maneuvers or something and make me divert to Mansfield!" It was his favourite punishment. He was getting annoyed.

"Come on! Let's do it!"

"Uh, uh." I was adamant. Later, on the ground, I'd asked him if he was trying to trick me.

"No," he'd smiled, "I was just curious to see what effect flaps and slip would have. Really. We were at four thousand feet, you know. Perfectly safe." Doug. You had to love him.

The nosewheel lifted off the centre stripe, or so Doug told me, and to my delight and surprise we were airborne. I had done it on instruments. At 1,400 feet, I started a turn to the left and the barrel DG rotated to the right. That's what it was supposed to do and that's why they were so unpopular.

"Just one request," I commented as we left the circuit, "let's not divert to Mansfield."

"I thought you loved Mansfield," Doug laughed, knowing full well how much trouble I'd had finding the rural aerodrome the previous July. Not this time. This was all business, this instrument flying. It took much more concentration than visual flying and left little time to chatter with Doug, much as I would have liked.

You didn't need actual night for night endorsement hood work. I couldn't see outside under the hood. After the required five hours on instruments, I was pumped to fly at night. I had heard how lovely night flying could be but not how inconvenient

141

it was to take the training in mid-July when night didn't arrive until nine o'clock, or later. Every evening in the BFC lobby, Doug and I would play out the same scene.

"Looks dark enough to me," I said, whining a little.

"It's not night," replied Doug, flatly and firmly. I hadn't anticipated this problem. Not only did I have to wait all day to go flying, I had to decline intoxicating spirits all day. In July, yet! Long days at the beach and no beer. Barbecues in the backyard and no beer. Old friends visiting and no beer. Sigh.

"It is officially night," Doug pronounced, checking the clock on the wall. "Let's go."

Not much to this, I thought, as we lifted off and headed into the circuit for some touch-and-goes.

"Pretty much like day-time, so far," I mused, as we entered the downwind for three-three. But what a view! You could see for a hundred miles! And lights! Lights everywhere, some of them moving. "Are those all...?"

"Airplanes?" Doug finished for me. "Yes they are. You can see them a lot better at night. Some are landing at Pearson, some Toronto Island, then there's Burlington, King City, Buttonville and here. Some are just heading right on through. Now pay attention here, you have to get the right angle of descent," he cautioned as I turned final.

"No problem," I replied, but in truth it was becoming a bit of a problem. Below me was a black void with no hint of perspective. Ahead, the runway lights created a long receding rhombus and the lights were my only gauge of altitude.

"Check your altimeter." The voice came out of the black.

Altimeter! Right, I thought, I do have one of those. Hmmm, a little low. Oops! I guess I said that out loud.

"You can't be a little low at night lest the unseen earth rise up and smite thee," Doug incanted, as I added power and lots of it. The threshold appeared and I sensed I was home free. All I had to do was grease it onto that strip of black between those two rows of lights. I'll show this guy how much my landings have improved, I thought.

Wham! Then wham again!

"What the...!" I exclaimed, as UPX finished its last bounce after dropping the final two feet onto the runway from a full stall. How the heck are you supposed to judge the flare over a black runway at night? I wondered.

"You've hung on to your unique technique, I see!" Doug laughed, remembering some of the stinkers I had pulled off the year before. But before I could argue he added, "Landing at night is a lot trickier than you might have thought. That's why we have to train you," he said in exaggerated soothing tones. "Don't worry, soon you'll land at night as well as you do by day."

There was something about that last statement that grated, but we were already blasting off for another circuit and I was determined to nail the next landing. It wasn't much smoother than the first one, but I was learning.

I had valid reasons for doing this in the first place and it wouldn't have done any good to get the endorsement if I weren't proficient, not that Doug would give it to me in that case anyway. This night endorsement wasn't just more black ink on my ticket. I planned to use it. Back home, the winter days were shorter than a three martini lunch and the previous winter there had been some tense moments trying to get home before dark.

In spite of my forced sobriety, the long days waiting for night to fall were not entirely wasted. Happily, I filled them with fan flights. Among the grinning passengers that summer was Michael of the Virginia Falls adventure, and his friend, Ross.

Papa X-Ray was claiming its victims. After a few flights on those perfect summer days, both Michael and Ross were smitten. I knew the symptoms. This was aviationitis. Advanced stages. Michael and Ross promptly signed up for flight training and they wanted to complete it in their own plane, just like their friend, Jim had done. What had I started?

For the three of us, flying was a disease. Its symptoms included sweaty palms, perspiring foreheads, blank stares and distorted perception. There was no cure, although more than one victim cleverly masked the symptoms in the interest of marital harmony. All one could do was treat the symptoms. First, Michael and Ross had to buy a plane and not just any plane would do. It had to be cheap.

"How cheap?" I asked.

"How much do airplanes cost?" asked one.

How much do airplanes cost? Where to start?

The perceptual changes brought on by advanced aviationitis should not be underestimated. To one pilot, his plane was a flying chariot, a gleaming thing of beauty with a soul of its own. To another it was just another TriPacer. I began poking around BFC looking for something in the economy range for Ross and Michael. Suddenly one day, there it was, a 1965 Cessna 172, with an O-300 engine. I walked them up to it one blistering afternoon.

"It's just an old 172," I said. "You're not going to get much of a plane for what you're willing to pay, you know…" My words were falling on deaf ears. To these two city boys it was the prettiest little airplane they had ever laid their eyes on. It had everything: wings, engine and the right price. The other facts were minor, according to Ross and Michael.

Although the engine had lots of time left to overhaul, the airframe had long since accumulated eight thousand hours, *eight* thousand. In fact, it did not appear to everyone to be a thing of unqualified pulchritude. The red and black paint was long past prime and well into the primer.

"Elbow grease, that's all she'll take," said Michael, eyes glistening, hands caressing the faded red and black paint.

CF-SLD had been stored in a barn for some time and, although one could understand and forgive the layer of guano under the engine cowl, the straw and other evidence of small animal life within the cabin was a bit disturbing. The radio, on the other hand, worked as well as those twenty-three-year-old radios did, on all ninety channels.

"We'll pick up a new radio, no problem," said Ross.

"The price is right," said Michael.

They bought the plane. Aviationitis had claimed two more victims. Sandwiched between discussions of annual inspections and steel versus Cermichrome cylinders, Michael informed me that he had left broadcasting to start his own company.

"It's the perfect location," he cooed, applying a second coat of wax to SLD's tired old paint. "We've set up shop right beside Runway three-three at Buttonville," he added, standing back to survey his work. SLD was beginning to look, well, better. He looked at me, intently. "You know, Jim, we're making videos over there. You're not going to stay in the north forever so why don't you think about producing some educational videos with us?"

"It sounds intriguing," I replied. "The fact that I know absolutely nothing about producing videos isn't a problem then?"

"You'll learn from the best, Sport!" Michael slapped my back. "I can teach ya all ya need to learn." I helped him gather his polishing rags and assorted wax potions as the idea of video production began to work on me.

"But, what kind of videos could I make? The possibilities are endless," I protested, weakly.

Papa X-Ray on one of several Lang trips through the Rocky Mountains of British Columbia.

Father Mary, the Catholic priest who called the Nahanni River settlements his parish. Father Mary was a frequent passenger in Papa X-Ray, sometimes carrying more than spiritual guidance.

Author Jim Lang visually checks the fuel before a training flight at the Brampton Flying Club (near Toronto, Ontario).

Virginia Falls, twice as high as Niagara, thunders below Papa X-Ray's wing.

Jim Lang and Papa X-Ray at Nahanni Butte, circa 1987.

Lang's students gather to help with the move out and bid the family goodbye.

The Lang family, John, Mary and Jim, September, 1998 in front of their latest airplane.

"Well," he replied, "how about something to do with economics? I'll bet there's not much of that in the schools these days." He stopped. "Look, why don't you do some research and then fly into Buttonville next week? I'll have somebody pick you up at the terminal."

The next day, Mary, Johnny and I got out of Olive's Dodge, which I had just parked one street behind the Ontario Institute for Studies in Education.

"It's a beautiful day," Mary said. "I'll just take Johnny for a walk out here. You go on and do what you have to do." I agreed and trotted into the library.

This felt all too familiar. I hadn't been here since '72 when I had run screaming from a Ph.D. program in philosophy. The ghost of grad school past fluttered by, sending a small shiver down my spine.

"May I help you?" a pleasant voice broke my concentration. I was scanning row after row of books, searching for economics. I looked up into the face of the librarian who, amazingly, appeared exactly like the stereotype of a librarian, complete with glasses and hair tied back neatly in a bun.

"Oh, hello!" I stammered. "Yes, I'm trying to find out what kind of economics courses are taught in high school."

"Oh, well, then," she said, "all you have to do is go up to the eighth floor. There's a foundation that knows all about that kind of thing. It's called The Canadian Foundation for Economic Education."

Upstairs, a smiling, motherly woman greeted me and listened as I explained the reason for my visit. "Our Executive Director isn't here today, so why don't you see Stephanie, down the hall? I'll tell her to expect you."

Later, in Stephanie's office, I learned that the foundation – CFEE, as it's better known – had recently commissioned a booklet entitled, *"Entrepreneurship, A Primer for Canadians."* I leafed through it and was immediately gripped with the feeling that I'd found what I was looking for.

"Do you people ever make videos?" I asked.

"We surely do," Stephanie replied, laughing.

"Then, if I can take this booklet, I'll be back in touch with you," I replied.

I found Mary and Johnny lying among flowers in the green grass near Olive's car. We scanned the booklet together. "Isn't this amazing stuff?" I enthused. "It's like a description of what you and I have done for years, especially in the music business."

"I didn't know there was 'entrepreneurship'," Mary added. "And yet, that's what we've been doing. We were entrepreneurs and didn't even know it."

"Look at this," I said, flipping through the pages. "Six chapters will nicely make six videos. I've got to talk to Michael!"

Instead of waiting around for dark the next day, I jumped into Papa X-Ray and blasted off for Buttonville. I tracked across the top of Toronto, past Bolton, Highway 400 and onto Highway 404 then headed south. I dialed up 124.8. This was my first flight to Buttonville and I was now discovering that it could be hard to find in the summer haze.

"Buttonville tower, Uniform Papa X-Ray, over."

"UPX, Buttonville, go ahead."

"Buttonville, UPX, 172, out of Brampton for Buttonville, now at two thousand feet somewhere north of you, over."

"UPX, Buttonville, are you familiar with the field, over?"

"Negative. Where the heck are you?" A small chuckle filled my headset.

"Just follow the 404 south and you'll find yourself on final for one-five. Call me when you're three miles out."

I flew on into the thick white haze. How do these people fly in this? I wondered. You didn't see this kind of meteorological phenomenon north of sixty degrees latitude, that's for sure. I flicked on my landing light and stared into the murk ahead.

"Papa X-Ray, Buttonville tower, do you have the field in sight, over?"

"Negative. But I have the 404 directly below me.."

"Fine, just keep on coming, you'll see the field off to your left." No sooner had the words left his mouth when a huge runway appeared directly ahead. I was less than half a mile on final and didn't even know it.

"I have the field, Buttonville and I appear to be on short final, but kinda high, over."

"UPX, cleared to land one-five."

"Papa X-Ray, cleared to land," I repeated, as I stood on the right rudder and pulled off a slip that would have made Doug Hannah proud. I dropped like a rock to three hundred feet, slapped on forty degrees of flap and set Papa X-Ray down like a feather just beyond the numbers. Take that, you city-slickers, I thought.

A shiny new black Chevy rolled up to the door minutes after my call to Michael. A knock-out, drop-dead blond stepped out and asked, "Are you Jim Lang?"

"If I wasn't before, I am now," I replied, knowing that Mary would want me to show some appreciation for such eye-popping beauty. Jackie, Michael's new assistant and office manager, turned out to be as sharp and delightful as she looked. The drive, however, was far too short. In fact, we simply backtracked Runway three-three to arrive at Michael's office. As I stepped out of the car, I could have tossed a rock and hit several planes taxiing off the runway which ran right past his building. This was beginning to look like a trap, set to catch northern aviators.

It got worse. Inside the building, it was clear Michael was gearing up for some serious business. Only three or four of what would become a staff of more than thirty professionals bustled about the new premises. I was ushered to Michael's corner office. I noticed that his office furniture, from desk to chair to coffee table, was the latest design from Ross' furniture manufacturing business. Looks like the partners in SLD were doing business on more than one plane. Above Michael's head, a battery-powered model of a Cessna Centurian hummed in an endless steep turn. He was bitten very badly. I almost felt sorry for him. I showed him my ideas for a video series based on entrepreneurs.

"I love it, Lang!" he exclaimed. "Let's do it! I'll get the wheels moving here and you go finish your night ticket and then get yourself back up north. I'll call you when we're ready to launch the project."

As I flew back to Brampton, I began to wonder just what I was getting myself into this time. What if he really did call? I'd have to quit my job as principal. Move to Toronto? Shudder. Oh, well, I concluded, as I taxied off one-five at Brampton, I've lived long enough to know that deals like these almost always fall through. No point in getting too excited about it at this stage of the game.

That evening, the dim red glow of the instrument lights warmed the cozy cockpit as Doug Hanna and I floated above the Ontario heartland. "It's like being in outer space, Doug," I breathed over the intercom. The lights below were all we could see of the houses and streets. The ground was invisible and you could pretend that nothing but empty space extended beyond the lights. The sensation was remarkable.

147

Night navigation proved to be easier than flying by day as distant cities and lighted towers could be seen for miles and miles. Mansfield, to my knowledge, was mercifully, not lighted. My landings improved as I learned to hold a consistent approach and even Doug had to admit I finished better than I had started.

"You're on your own," Doug said a few nights later. "Just fly off a couple more hours in the circuit and check with Rick Wynott." And that was that.

It was over so soon, logbook stamped, goodbyes said. Summer was over too. Time to head back to Nahanni Butte, our fourth full "cross-the-country" trip in a year. But this time there would be no more fear of nightfall. I pulled Papa X-Ray onto the threshold of three-three and turned to the little family.

"Let's go," said Mary, strapping on her headset. Was that a smile?

"When are we going to get there Dad?" asked young Johnny, strapped into his car seat behind me. At four, he was already a veteran back-seat flyer. No evidence of aviationitis there, I thought, as I firewalled the trusty old Continental.

By now the trip north was becoming almost ordinary so we broke from tradition and took the American route south of Lake Superior. New names and places were added to Papa X-Ray's logbook. We spent the first night at Ashland, Wisconsin, fueled up in Duluth, Bimidji and Grand Rapids, Minnesota and then we forged on past Devil's Lake and settled into our second night at Minot, North Dakota. Everywhere we stopped in the United States we were treated royally and we vowed to take this route whenever possible.

Back in Canada the next day, we began to join the now familiar dots that tracked back to Nahanni Butte. I used my new night endorsement for a landing in Red Deer, Alberta.

"Look, Johnny," Mary poked him in the back seat, "look! You can see the lights of Edmonton, Red Deer and all the way to Calgary. Isn't it beautiful?"

"Yeah, beautiful!" Johnny repeated, perhaps meaning it, perhaps learning to just go along with this enthusiasm thing his parents seemed to have about flying.

"Johnny, look, there!" Mary pointed to a small patch of lights south of Red Deer. "There's Penhold, where we used to live and see just past that, those lights? That's Innisfail where you were born."

"Yeah, I was born!" Johnny echoed, in exactly the same tone as before.

Fortunately, my landings had improved to the point that Mary felt nothing unusual in our touchdown at Penhold, where the Red Deer Airport was located. We were joined by our good friends Rob, Melinda and their growing family and spent an evening reminiscing about the days when Rob, Mary and I were a trio in the music business. The next morning, I took Rob and his two sons, William and Quinn, for a short traditional, fan flight. Melinda watched from the ground, smiling a secret little smile. A few months later, to our delight and surprise, she gave birth to little Lauren.

The next day it was on to Grande Prairie, Fort St. John and, our home away from home, Fort Nelson. We topped off what was left of our luggage space with fresh vegetables, spent the night in a motel and settled into the final leg first thing the next morning. As the Butte came into sight, I felt it was time to consider the new Continental officially "broken in." I throttled back to a more economical power setting. There. I'd flown her hard, just like I had been told to do.

"Oh, it's good to be home again," Mary said, as I descended for the Nahanni strip.

"But for how long?" I replied, knowing that a call from Michael could make this our last return trip ever. A few minutes later I killed the ignition in front of our log house. We stepped out into a cloud of hungry mosquitoes and a small throng of welcoming students.

# Chapter Sixteen

# Good company

The fall of '87 turned out to be chock full of flying. As I met more and more commercial bush jockeys, I was grateful to be able to carry on a slightly more intelligent conversation with them than I had two years before. In turn, they offered understated respect for the fact that I'd not yet killed myself and they appreciated the fact that I didn't "chisel-charter", taking business away from their operations with Papa X-Ray. Although UPX stayed busy all fall, I had more than the usual number of opportunities to ride with the pros and to critique their flying for a change.

The new school year got off to a roaring start. No sooner had the kids been organized into their new grades, textbooks handed out and pencils sharpened when...

"Come quick! Come quick! Albert fell and won't get up!" shouted Morgan, one of my Grade Four students as he raced into the school one afternoon during recess.

"Where is he?" I asked, grabbing my jacket and heading for the door.

"On the road! Follow me!" the little fellow shouted excitedly, racing back out the door. Emergencies were not uncommon in Nahanni Butte and, for reasons I've never completely understood, the teacher was usually the first person called to the scene.

I ran through the schoolyard, past the Band Office and out to the road. About a hundred yards ahead I saw a small group of people standing around on the dirt-path that lead from the airstrip to the village. I arrived, puffing, and bent over the middle-aged man lying beside an overturned three-wheeler. This was bad, I quickly realized, as I examined the victim's already-swollen and bashed face.

"Call for medevac!" I instructed one of the onlookers, who quickly started toward the nursing station to radio Fort Simpson.

Then he stopped, as another said, "We already radioed in from the nursing station. The doctor is on his way."

I was aware of women crying and moaning around me as I tried to take control of the situation. I was not medically trained but then, no one else was either and somebody had to do something.

"Is he...?" somebody asked, from behind my shoulder.

"No, he's not dead but he's not good either," I said, noting his laboured breathing. I took his pulse. It was more than 140, not good but it seemed strong enough. He began to stir. With the movement I caught a strong whiff of alcohol. It appeared this accident had extenuating circumstances.

"Don't move, Albert," I said. "You'll be all right but don't move because I don't know what you've broken, if anything." He struggled briefly, then relaxed into unconsciousness once more. With help from his sister, now bending over him with me, we gently lifted his swelling head and put a coat under it to protect him from the stones and gravel. Then we covered him with another coat. I realized I could do no more than monitor his pulse and breathing until the plane arrived with the doctor, which it did, an hour later.

"You'd better come with me to Fort Nelson," Martin, the young pilot, said as we helped the doctor load Albert onto a stretcher and into the waiting 207. "I can't take a delirious stretcher case all the way with only one body to attend."

"Morgan," I instructed the wide-eyed little boy who continued to hover around the scene, "tell Mary I won't be home until dark, okay?"

"Okay, Mr. Lang!" he said, running off in the direction of my house.

The 207 climbed out effortlessly with the light load and soon we were cruising south at 2,500 feet over the bush. From the copilot seat I glanced back to see the doctor changing the IV. With the seats removed the long plane was well suited to the purpose and the doctor had plenty of room beside the stretcher to attend to his patient, who now slumbered peacefully.

"Here, take this," the doctor said, handing me a half-full IV bag.

"What is it?" I asked, taking the plastic bag gingerly.

"Saline...salt water," he replied, "you can get rid of it. I've started another one."

I sat there with the dripping bag in my hands and began to look around for a place to dump it. Nothing. I looked down. Primeval forest. I caught Martin's eye, indicated the bag and then looked down to the bush. He smiled and eased back on the throttle, then said, "Go for it!"

I cracked the window and slipped the bag through the opening where it quickly disappeared below the wheels. I suppose we could have been reported for unauthorized dumping from a plane but this was wild, unpopulated country. It would have been a particularly unlucky moose who positioned himself in the path of the ballistic IV.

We transferred our patient to a waiting ambulance in Fort Nelson. Meanwhile, the doctor had bones to saw back in Fort Simpson and I had to get home to Nahanni. Since Nahanni was more or less on the way, we headed there first. Unfortunately, it was already getting dark when we arrived back. The doctor was forced to get off the plane with me while Martin flew it back to Simpson.

"Can't fly commercial after dark," Martin explained. "Sorry, Doc. I'll come back for you tomorrow."

"Where the heck were you?" asked Mary when the doctor and I stumbled through the doorway.

"Didn't Morgan tell you?" I asked.

"He said something about you being gone until dark but I didn't know where or why."

"Well, I'll let the doctor explain. Oh by the way, he'll be staying over and we are some hungry," I said, introducing the young physician. "How about Moose teriyaki?" I suggested to the good doctor. "I should warn you that I'm the cook in this household!"

"Sounds great," he replied.

"Moose teriyaki coming up, hold the saline." We laughed, remembering the bag of salt water, now resting somewhere on the forest floor, or on a moose's antlers.

Early into the school year, people at the Department of Education, who were much smarter than me and my fellow rural principals, decided that if we were to act as principals we ought to be certified as such. We showed up in Yellowknife that October and dutifully began the certification course. I had more mixed feelings than most, as I expected to have to cut my new career short before the year was up. But I enjoyed the chance to rub shoulders with my colleagues and get in an occasional game of poker at the same time.

Our heads stuffed with important new knowledge, we headed back to our respective turfs aboard a vintage Douglas DC-3. The flight was a treat. As my fellow travelers eyed the old bird skeptically, I was in my glory. Wow, my first ride in a Three. I loved the drone of the big old radial engines and there was plenty of time to savor it. The trip to Fort Simpson normally took about an hour and a half in the old transport.

"This is the captain speaking. We've encountered quite a headwind so we're going to be an hour late arriving in Simpson. Enjoy the flight."

Must be quite a headwind, I thought, to add a whole hour. No matter, more time to soak in the experience. Sure enough, a full hour late, we touched down at the DOT strip. The tail settled back and we taxied in, nose pointed proudly to the sky. As we transferred to the waiting vans that would shuttle us to the town runway, the weather appeared to be coming down.

By the time we reached the ramp at Simpson, the weather was marginal VFR at best. The ragged, wintry ceiling threatened to brush the treetops that bordered the gravel strip. When the last of the boxes and suitcases were unceremoniously dumped into the cargo area of the big Twin Otter, our pilot casually ambled toward the plane, his heavy boot grinding out the last of a cigarette without missing a step.

"We'll give Trout Lake a try first," he told the group of principals, busily strapping themselves into the passenger seats, as he threaded his way up the aisle to the cockpit. Dark, lithe and handsome, with a Clark Gable mustache accentuating his weather-beaten face, Bob was every inch the image of the northern pilot. Not that any of the mildly nervous passengers cared a whit about Gable. They just wanted to get home in one piece and that meant getting to Fort Liard, Trout Lake and Nahanni Butte in whatever order worked.

I took a seat near the front so I could peek into the cockpit to watch a pro at work. I was sure we would soon be back on the ground here at Simpson, forced down by the weather. Had it been my decision, I never would have attempted the trip. But my limits weren't everybody's limits and I knew Bob didn't get to the shady side of fifty by making serious mistakes. As the Twin Otter rumbled into the gray afternoon, I observed Bob's cool detachment, driving the airplane like a family station wagon.

153

Forehead pressed against the window, I peered out at the worsening conditions, noting the tree tops about a thousand feet below our fat tundra tires. A tap on my shoulder distracted me and I turned to see a grim-faced colleague.

"Is this guy crazy or what?" he asked, clearly not as confident in our captain as I was.

"He may very well be crazy," I answered, "but he didn't live this long by being stupid. He'll turn back if he has to and besides, this is an IFR twin so we can always land at the DOT strip if necessary," I comforted him.

"Yeah?" he asked again, his fear dissolving into mere uncertainty.

"Trust me. We all want to live as much as you do," I said firmly, but politely. Why was it that nervous passengers always assumed they were the only ones who valued life? Didn't they know that pilots wanted to die quietly in their beds at a ripe old age just like everyone else? At least, I certainly hoped they did.

Five hundred feet and maybe two miles visibility, that's what I made it from my side of the plane. I glanced up to the cockpit in time to see Bob peel the cellophane from a new pack of Players Plain, crack the cockpit window a half-inch and feed the wrapping to the slipstream outside. Not exactly Kosher, but old habits die hard. As Bob lit a fresh smoke, I checked conditions again. I'd turn back here, I said to myself, noting our altitude had dropped another hundred feet or so. Clumps of scud now fluffed past the window and visibility had dropped to vertical when I felt the big plane begin a left-hand one-eighty degree turn.

"Back to Simpson," I said to my nervous companion, anticipating his question. "At least we gave it a try."

I squinted, scanning the panel ahead for information about our destination. Simpson would have been north by northeast but the heading indicator clearly pointed northwest. What's going on here...?

Bob offered nary a clue. As the ceiling rose a few hundred feet and the puffs of stratus thinned a bit, he handed control to his copilot. Then he casually picked up his paperback novel and began to read. Almost on cue, the sky lifted and we were a few miles back of Nahanni Butte. With no more than a nod to his right and a firm, "I have control," Bob set the big bird down on the narrow Nahanni strip and taxied right into the village. With the left prop in beta mode, he pivoted the twin on a dime, the clearance lights missing both store and nursing station by more than two feet. Then he jumped out and lit another Player's. All in a day's work. I tipped my hat to him and headed for the house.

"Guess what?" Mary said, by way of greeting. "While you were gone, we were invited to play some tunes at the next Christmas party in Fort Simpson. I said, 'yes'."

I gulped. "Well, we've got some serious practising to do then," I replied, examining my fingertips for any trace of calluses that might not have vanished since I'd last played guitar.

"They'll even fly us in, they said," she added, knowing that might sway me a little more. I guessed she'd been practising her fiddle a little more than I had my guitar, as she seemed quite eager to get back on the stage after two and a half years.

"Okay," I said, "if you've already agreed, I guess there's nothing I can do but start practising. Do you remember how to play Orange Blossom Special?"

"After three thousand performances, how could I ever forget?" she laughed.

Two months later, it was time to put up or shut up. We hitched a ride to Simpson with Paul Jones in Simpson Air's Twin Otter. We were delighted to spend time with Paul and Margaret, not just because they were good friends, but they also shared our taste in music. At least Paul did and as a veteran northern aviator, he could hangar fly with me until the cows came home.

The King Air, Twin Otter and assorted 185s Paul flew for hire didn't quite satisfy his desire to own his own plane. Unlike me, he didn't go too far afield so he'd bought the only available plane in Fort Simpson, a 1958 Cessna 172. It was polished aluminum and green and it was his little baby. We spent the early evening arguing the merits of his O-300 versus mine while we chowed down on roast caribou and sipped a little distilled spirits before heading over to the hall for the evening show.

As we stepped into the room, I felt a sudden attack of stage fright. Three hundred people turned to watch Mary and me walk up to the front. "Um, I hope we're up for this," I mumbled to her. Johnny traipsed alongside, oblivious to the crowd and the pre-show din they sent up, chattering and visiting as only northerners can.

George Tuckaroo emceed the evening, kicking it off with a wild impersonation of "dance styles among the Dene". Well-known throughout the north, George was a regular media personality and a professional comic in his own right.

155

"Thank goodness for George," I breathed to Mary, as we waited in the wings. "I'm glad we didn't have to carry the whole show ourselves."

Before she could answer, we heard George begin our introduction. "All the way from Nahanni Butte, Lang & Ackroyd!" We hit the stage running — and singing!

"Ridin' the night on a hard cold wind
On the trail of the long lonesome pine
Thinkin' of you, feelin' so blue
Wondrin' why I left you behind..."

The old tunes came back as though we'd never left the business. It was just like the old days with one small exception. Throughout our bluegrass set, a chubby young boy kept tugging at my leg.

"Can I sing now, Dad? I want to sing now!" Johnny was pleading. The crowd loved it, thinking it was part of the show. I realized we had become a trio and was delighted to give the audience what they wanted. I dragged over a chair. Johnny jumped up and standing on his toes was just able to reach the mike.

"Ready? One, two , three..."

"You are my sunshine, my only sunshine..." he launched into his favourite two-tune medley, finishing up with, "Let the Sunshine In". The crowd ate it up. By the time we kicked into our closing "Orange Blossom Special", Johnny was getting right into his new-found popularity. He danced his way through the whole tune and drew bigger applause than we'd ever received for this old chestnut in the ten years we'd performed it around the world. His career was short-lived, however, as he discovered "shyness" a few months later and never fully recovered.

"I had fun," I said to Mary the next day, as we headed for the strip in Paul's truck.

"I thought we were pretty rusty," she replied, "but it was fun, wasn't it?"

"Hey, you guys were great!" Paul assured her. "Such talent hiding out in Nahanni Butte," he tsk-tsked. At the strip we loaded up Paul's old 172 and squeezed in for the ride home.

"How much do you bet I can get her in the air by the second marker?" Paul asked as we taxied to position.

"Five bucks of easy money," I responded, taking the bet. We shook on it. He might have a lot more experience than me, I thought, but it's still a straight-tail '58 172 with a tired engine and we're stretching gross weight. I glanced back at wife and child, guitar and baggage, and then over to Paul, who was at least as heavy as my two hundred pounds. No way, I thought. We'll be lucky to get off at all let alone in three hundred feet.

Paul stood on the brakes and ran the little O-300 up to full power before letting the aging kite lumber forward. It seemed I could have walked faster than we were traveling when we approached the appointed marker.

I've won! I thought. That very second, he grasped the Johnson-bar flap lever with one hand and gave it an unearthly heave. With the other he yanked back on the yoke, hauling the unwilling plane into the air. There it hovered, stall horn squawking and wings wobbling in ground effect like a new-born colt. Then, inches above the gravel, we slowly built up speed and, by mid-strip, began a painful climb out.

"I didn't say how high I'd get her into the air, did I?" he said, laughing, as I conceded the bet. After almost three years up here, I'm still learning new tricks from these guys, I thought.

Back on the ground at Nahanni, we waved goodbye to Paul and dragged our guitars and the newest member of our band into the house. We were just in time to hear the radiophone start squawking.

"Yeah, is this Jim Lang, over?" A familiar voice emerged through the crackle and hiss. "Michael, is that you, over?"

"Lang, you old bushpilot! Are you ready to change careers?"

"You mean…"

"The entrepreneurship video series project got the green light. Now get down here and help me make the thing." My heart jumped and sank almost simultaneously.

Nolan, my new superintendent, reacted wonderfully to my plea for a release from my contract. I agreed to find a replacement, which I managed to do, and he agreed to provide a letter from the Department allowing me to go with their blessing. In fact, they'd pay my way out, just as they'd paid my way in. Now, these are good people, I thought.

I was elated to be able to take on the exciting new work but I was saddened to leave the north. It had taken quite a hold on me.

Mary, on the other hand, thought it was time to go. "It's been great," she said, "but you and I know we're really southerners and will always be southerners. Might as well take the opportunity while we can." And with that she promptly began selling off our household possessions to anyone and everyone in the village.

"Why drag this stuff south when these people can make good use of it here?" she asked, rhetorically.

The good citizens of Nahanni agreed. This was an opportunity for us to lighten our load and for them to get a good deal on everything from my Ski-Doo, which Raymond bought, to my Browning .308, picked up by James. Nobody wanted the microwave, however. "Too strange," Laura said. "We're not used to them." When the Twin Otter arrived to carry out what was left, we could scarcely fill a third of the cargo hold.

My last day at school was emotional. I said goodbye to Laura, my faithful classroom assistant who had saved me from myself more times than I cared to remember. I posed with the kids for one last photo and said goodbye to everyone. We would be taking off at first light the next morning. Everyone would be asleep when we left.

# Chapter Seventeen

# One-way ticket south

"I won't wake her up. I'll just leave the stuff on her doorstep," I said to Mary, as I picked up two boxes of perishables from our now empty fridge and stepped out into the black, cold, early morning air. We were the only life stirring in the settlement. I stopped outside our house and cocked my head toward UPX, parked beside the nursing station. A faint hum emanated from the blanketed 172 and I was satisfied that the pre-heater was doing its job one last time.

Mukluks squeaking on the cold snow, I trundled over to Laura's house. We were leaving her all the food we wouldn't be able to take with us. We had become good friends with Laura and Raymond and we would miss them more than anyone, except maybe for Elsie, Laura's mother, who had made all our moccasins and mukluks. I set the box down gently outside the door and shuffled back to our house for another load.

Mary was bundled into her winter wardrobe when I returned. "Better get this garbage burned," she said, as she dragged several old boxes out to the incinerator across the road. When I passed by laden with more boxes of ketchup, lard and frozen milk, the yellow flames were already crackling and snapping in the cold air, boring a bright hole in the black morning

Johnny greeted us as we clambered back into the house one last time. "Are we going now?" the little pajama-clad figure asked through lazy yawns.

"Yes, we are, sweetie," Mary said, hustling him out of the cold draft and into his room to change.

"We're going to Grandma's?" he asked.

"Both Grandmas," Mary answered. "First we'll see Grandma and Grandpa Lang in Regina and then we'll see Grandma Ackroyd in Brampton. And we'll live with her for a while."

By now we were experts at loading the plane. As I began to shuffle the bags and suitcases in the direction of UPX, I still couldn't quite believe we were actually leaving. Ten minutes later, it was all done and the eastern sky was now light enough for take-off. With mixed feelings of excitement and sadness, we taxied down to the strip one last time, pointed UPX south and sailed into the morning light.

"Goodbye, Nahanni Butte," Mary said, as I dipped a wing for one last look at the little village. How tiny it was. Just a few scattered cabins, the school and the store, their little chimneys sending ribbons of white smoke up toward us as we climbed away from the river and the Butte beyond. It would be the third time we had flown between this little corner of the Northwest Territories and Brampton. Four trips, counting the returns. But this one had no return booked. It was one-way only.

Except for some wet armpits near Fort St. John where the visibility and the ceiling dropped and rose like a foggy curtain, it was a textbook trip to Regina, our first family stop. As Dad wheeled the big Chrysler into the parking lot at Guy's Aviation Esso, he looked much older than his seventy-eight years. This was a time of new beginnings and more goodbyes than we had counted on. I guess we all sensed that Dad wasn't well as the whole clan had gathered for a late Christmas reunion. The table creaked, over-laden with food, and brother-in-law Barry regaled the crowd with animated stories from his youth in the streets of post-war London. We all posed for pictures, Dad and Mom front and centre. And we all cried when we said goodbye to the rest of the family.

Dad drove us to the airport. As we made the turn off Lewvan Drive, I felt it was time to speak up. "Dad, you know when the house gets to be too much for you and mom, just hire a house-keeper. You don't have to try to do everything yourselves, you know."

"Oh, well," he replied, chuckling, "I don't think that's going to come up, frankly. I don't think I'm going to be around that much longer." I wasn't surprised to hear him say that, as he was always making cracks about having already had his "three score years and ten."

"I'm on bonus years, now, boy!" he'd say.

He dropped us at the Esso. As we embraced and parted, we knew this would be our last goodbye. His eyes said it all. Three months later, after a series of short, increasingly severe strokes, he died. To this day I have trouble keeping a dry eye at Guy's Esso, the last place I saw my father alive.

A howling northwesterly pushed us along at breakneck speed toward Minot, our first scheduled fuel stop after Regina. But the visibility began to drop in an icy haze and it appeared nature wasn't going to let us go that easily. Ten miles from Magic City, as the locals prefer to call Minot, I descended to a thousand feet and cranked UPX around in a bumpy one-eighty turn. The visibility had dropped to less than a mile and the wind continued to howl. I rotated above a small village in a broad valley and reached for the radio.

"Magic City tower, Uniform Papa X-Ray, over."

"Canadian Uniform X-Ray Papa," the voice returned, confused as always by the phonetic registration, "Magic City tower, go ahead."

"Roger Magic City tower, Uniform Papa X-Ray ten north at one thousand feet squawking twelve hundred. We're on a VFR flight plan bound for customs at Minot but are holding ten north for weather, over."

"Papa X-Ray, roger, Magic City conditions are VFR at the moment. Can you file IFR to get in, over?"

"Magic City, Papa X-Ray, negative. VFR rated only, over."

"Papa X-Ray, Magic City, say, we could turn you over to the military radar and they could steer you in, what do you say?"

"Let's give it a try." There was a short pause, then a new voice appeared.

"Uniform Papa X-Ray, this is Minot Radar, we have you radar identified ten northwest, would you like a steer to the field?"

"Sounds good, Minot. I'll call altitude if you'll look out for obstacles, over."

"Uniform Papa X-Ray squawk code four three five three, steer one six zero and maintain one thousand feet, over."

"Papa X-Ray," I answered, spinning the transponder knobs to the proper numbers. Radar hauled us in like a fish on a line and soon the field appeared off our right wing.

"Minot Tower, Uniform Papa X-Ray, I have the field in sight, and thank you."

"Roger Papa X-Ray, dial Magic City tower, squawk 1200 and have a nice day."

A nice day this was not and as I set UPX down in a forty-knot headwind the toughest part was yet to come, taxiing. With each turn on the taxiway a wing would threaten to lift and I fran-

tically tried to bring the nose into the gale to prevent going shiny-
side down. Fifteen minutes later we creaked to a stop outside
customs. This would be quick, I could tell, as the customs officer
braced himself against the wintry blast and approached my door.

"Anything to declare?" he hollered above the wind.

"I declare it is damn cold and windy!" I laughed, breaking my
own rule never to joke with border officials. But he laughed too
and asked us to join him inside where it was warmer.

I logged only one hour that day for the flying was over until
better weather arrived. We settled into our favourite motel just
across the street from the airport and hoped for clear skies the next
day. We were not to be disappointed. After a good night's rest, we
blasted off eastbound, into a crisp, clear morning.

Minot, Grand Forks, Bimidji and Grand Rapids, Minnesota,
the trek through the northern States had become familiar to us by
now, having passed this way only a few months before in the opposite direction. We were no longer startled by the enormous
communications tower thrusting into the prairie sky east of Minot.
We expected, and got, poor visibility passing Duluth which continued all the way to the Sault. It seemed too quick, somehow,
when our wheels touched down one more time at the Brampton
Flying Club.

"There's no such thing as a winter rating, if that's what you're
here for this time, Jim," said Rick Wynott, in greeting.

"Just a tie-down would do, thanks," I replied.

"Might have trouble there," the pretty desk clerk said.

"There were lots last summer," I objected.

"More airports have been shut down," she explained, "and
we're jammed with planes. But I think I can get you something
down at the EAA end of the field.

"I'll take what I can get, I guess," I said, just as my mother-in-
law's smiling face appeared, right on cue.

"Did you guys bring the cold weather?" Olive laughed, taking
her peck on the cheek from her son-in-law and daughter.

"Hey, what about me, me, me?" Johnny piped up. Olive gave
Johnny a big hug then helped Mary as she started to load the old
Dodge Monaco. I trotted back to the plane to find my tie-down
spot. Taxiing past the long rows of aircraft, I marveled at their
numbers and then marveled at my tie-down, far in the back behind
some suspicious experimental-type aircraft, in a gentle hollow on
the grass. Wheeling the little 172 between the two metal loops,

frozen into the ground, I wondered just how much I'd get to fly now that this new adventure had begun.

As I walked toward the clubhouse, I glanced back and was overtaken by a heavy sadness. She looked so ordinary here, just like the dozens of other 172s blanketing the field. Up north she was unique. She had a whole strip all to herself and proved a useful worthy workhorse. She had earned her keep.

"Can you handle rainbow trout for supper?" Olive asked as I settled in beside her in the big old car.

"Rainbow trout again?" I teased her as she swung the sedan out onto the highway. "Can you handle three more bodies in your house for a few months?" I countered.

"Will you do the cooking?" she laughed.

"Just point me to the kitchen," I responded as the happy carload disappeared into the bright lights of Brampton, just a little fainter than the brighter lights of the Toronto skyline, south on the horizon.

## Chapter Eighteen

# Cameron

"It's for you, Jim!" Olive called from the kitchen. I left Mary and Johnny at the table to take the phone.

"Hello?"

"Hi, Jim, it's Nick Sibbeston here."

I was floored. The leader of the government of the Northwest Territories was calling me? Here in Brampton? Nick was the MLA at Nahanni Butte and I'd met him a few times. He seemed kind and down-to-earth. An almost shy, unassuming man, for a politician, Mary had once addressed him as Mr. Patterson, his Minister of Education. And he didn't mind.

"Hi, Nick. This is an honour! What can I do for you?"

"I'd heard you'd moved down there, Jim, and I was just calling to see how you managed to do such a thing? I can't imagine moving from Nahanni Butte to Toronto. It's like going to the moon!"

I laughed. "Well Nick, I've been here many times before and to tell you the truth, I'm not sure how we'll manage it just yet either."

We chatted for a few more minutes and then I rejoined the family at the table. "Can you beat that?" I asked no one in particular. "I wonder if the Prime Minister would call if you moved to Florida, Olive?" I laughed.

Nick wasn't too far off the mark. It was a considerable adjustment for the three of us. Olive generously offered us a room in her house until we could find a place of our own, but the real estate market was in the middle of the biggest boom ever. Besides, Mary and I had managed to avoid living in cities for most of our lives and we didn't want to start now.

The drive from Buttonville to Brampton wasn't fun either. We bought an older Volvo and I began driving to work every day, just like every northerner's image of a southerner. Work on the entrepreneurship video project had started and that meant a one-hour commute, each way.

One Sunday in March, I drove up to the BFC to check on Papa X-Ray. My heart sank as I walked over to the faithful old 172. The tiedown area had flooded and then frozen. Her left wheel was nearly completely submerged under the ice. She sat at an uneven angle and looked altogether forlorn. Well, here you are, you schmuck, I said to myself. You're going to end up like every other glassy-eyed aviator who bought a plane and had to sell it for lack of use. It's just a matter of time. I drove back to Brampton more subdued than ever.

"Every problem is an opportunity, right?" Mary asked brightly. She laid the map of central Ontario on Olive's kitchen table. "And right now, our biggest problem is the fact that we can't afford to buy a house in Toronto, so..."

I saw where she was going with this. "So, if I'm commuting an hour through the city, why not commute from somewhere in the country, right?"

"Exactly, Jim," she answered, as her fingers started exploring the communities within a short drive of Toronto. She loved maps, that woman, and I was beginning to have more respect than ever for this little idiosyncrasy.

I scanned the area to the north and east of Toronto, checking for highways. I needed to have easy access, after all. Hmmm. Lots of possible places to live and some of them even have...airports.

"Mary, that's it! Airports! Let's look for a place that has a good airport. Then I could use Papa X-Ray to commute to Buttonville." Mary saw the point too. Instead of trying to find reasons to use the plane, we could move somewhere where we had to use it. Create a reason to fly just like we did at Nahanni.

"Okay, how far is a reasonable commute by 172?" I mused as I scanned the map. "Let's say about 75 miles."

"Why don't you just measure off that distance on this string, make an arc around Toronto and see what falls inside the arc?" Mary asked, handing me a piece of string. Olive was starting to take an interest now. No doubt she was about ready for us to find our own place. I put one end of the string on Buttonville and described an arc across the north and northeast.

"Stayner," Mary said. "It's near the cottage and it's within the arc. Wait, what about...Lindsay?"

"Never heard of it," I said, "but it looks like it has an airport near the town. And it's not too far away, either."

"Bob used to go fishing up Lindsay way," Olive piped up. "He used to love the pickerel they'd catch up there. And we had a premier from Lindsay, Leslie Frost. He was pretty good too. Lindsay's not nowhere, you know." she laughed.

"Okay, then it's settled. We'll check out Lindsay first."

Mary and I knew where we liked to live but we knew nothing about real estate. We had never owned a house. Michael, on the other hand, had bought and sold several houses. He'd even built a couple, including the one he was now living in, down in Toronto's beaches.

"Hey, Mike," I said the next day at his office, "want to go to Lindsay this weekend?"

"Lindsay? You mean the home of former premier Leslie Frost? That Lindsay?" he asked, quizzically.

"Okay, I guess everyone knew about Leslie Frost except me," I mumbled. "Yes, that Lindsay. We're thinking of moving there but we need to check out the airport and the local real estate first. Want to come?"

"You mean, fly to Lindsay? Count me in!"

On Sunday morning we left Johnny with his grandmother and took off for the Kawartha Lakes region full of towns with names like Bobcageon, Fenelon Falls, Burnt River, Coboconk and...Lindsay. After about forty minutes we were still looking for Lindsay.

"See anything, yet?"

"Nope. How can they hide a whole town like that? It's like Mansfield, for heaven's sake!"

"You had to divert to Mansfield, too, eh?" Michael laughed. I remembered that he had taken more than forty hours training at Brampton so he'd know Mansfield all right.

"There it is!" Mary shouted, pointing ahead and checking the chart in her lap. "Just have to look for Scugog over there and then over to Sturgeon Lake, over here," she pointed, "and Lindsay is right on that line between them, see?"

We saw. I flipped open the Flight Supplement and checked the numbers. "Wow! 3,500 feet paved!" I said to Michael, who was now studying the area intently.

I dialed in the Lindsay unicom frequency 122.8. Immediately a cacophony of transmissions filled my ears. Everyone from Ohio to Windsor was using this common small airport frequency it seemed. I waited for a break in the chatter and then fired off, "Lindsay Unicom, Uniform Papa X-Ray, over." Nothing. I tried

166

again. Nothing again. "Oh, well, I'll just do a normal approach to an uncontrolled aerodrome and get us down there," I said to Michael, who was utterly unconcerned.

I crossed the field at 2,500 feet eastbound for the turnaround when a Pitts Special came out of nowhere, inverted, and blew past our nose, slightly above us.

"Who was that?" I shouted. "What is that guy doing and where did he go?"

"There he is!" Mary pointed up, where the rogue was hanging on his tail in a hammerhead, then dropping and diving away to the west.

"Aircraft in the circuit at Lindsay," I radioed firmly, "state your intentions!" No answer. I looked over to see the culprit doing a wing-over then he landed on three-one. By the time I taxied in, he was parked and chatting with a couple of his pals. I got out of Papa X-Ray and made a beeline for him. "Excuse me," I said, catching his attention, "but do you have a radio in that thing?"

"Yeah, I do." He seemed unconcerned. "But, I don't bother to turn it on, why?"

"Why? Because you nearly killed us up there, that's why!"

"Oh, was that you in that 172? That wasn't close! Hell, I had you in sight all the time!"

"Well, I didn't have you in sight and I could just as easily have turned right into this nice little plane of yours. And what if there'd been a student up there? Next time, turn on your radio. And use it!" I stomped away. He seemed unimpressed. I heard later that he was busted for low flying over the crowd at an airshow. I wasn't surprised. I hoped his antics weren't an everyday occurrence at Lindsay.

We made our way to the tight little office where two smiling ladies behind the counter introduced themselves as Ann and Hilda. A clean-cut fellow stepped up and introduced himself as Neil, explaining that he and his girlfriend and her family owned and ran the place. We learned later that he flew left seat for Air Canada when he wasn't mucking around with more airplanes here. I thought, now there's a guy who can't seem to get enough of flying. My kinda guy.

"Do you get yahoos like that guy here a lot?" I asked, still a bit unnerved by the Pitts jockey.

"Oh, he's a bit strange, I admit," Neil replied, more than a trace of an accent hinting at British roots. "But he's not from here, no. Say, what brings you to Lindsay?"

"Well," I began, "we're thinking of moving here."

"Great," Ann said.

"Why?" asked Hilda.

"Well," Mary said, "you have a good airport for one thing and we were looking for a good airport…"

"We'd love to have more planes here," Neil chimed in. "We're planning a lot of improvements too."

"Tell me," Michael jumped in, "can you get a house around here for less than a hundred grand?" The women gave each other a look that defied translation. Must be a Lindsay look, I thought.

"I suppose," Hilda ventured, "depending on what you're looking for."

"Okay, then," I said, "which way to town?"

We decided to walk the short distance into Lindsay. It gave us a chance to check the place out. From Highway 35, we turned up Colbourne Street and then from Colbourne took a right down past the Town and Country Mall.

"Looks like a good supermarket, there," Mary said, pointing to the Loblaws.

Next we turned east on Kent, down into the centre of town and right up to a realty office. We stepped in and were greeted by an attractive blond woman.

"Hi, I'm Brenda," she said. "How can I help you?" An hour later we were scouting through some of her listings around Lindsay. I pretended to know what I was talking about, hoping Michael would save us from doing anything really stupid.

"Got anything a little less expensive?" I asked, as we piled back into her car.

"Well, there's a nice place out at Cameron," she began, "but it's a little north of here."

"Let's go."

Ten minutes later we were viewing a place on the eastern extremity of the tiny village. The two-storey house sat on a large, well-treed lot. Jean, the owner, was puffing on a smoke as we pulled up.

"Made it, eh?" She seemed like a tough old girl, but likable. Her house was immaculate. Three bedrooms upstairs and a nice big living room/dining room downstairs. We checked the basement.

"Smells like a furnace fuel leak down here," Michael said, ominously, all the while giving me a broad wink and a thumbs up.

He liked the place. I looked at Mary. She was smiling and grinning.

"We'll have our lawyer make you an offer," Michael announced as we drove off, our hearts pounding. A week later, we owned our very first house. Michael said it suited us perfectly. He was right. I called my folks to give them the good news. Dad answered the phone.

"Lindsay?" he chuckled, "Sure I know Lindsay. We had two fellas come out here during the "dirty Thirties" from Lindsay. They stooked oats for us for a few weeks. One of them was kinda sweet on my sister, Mary, if I recall." It seemed everyone knew about Lindsay except us.

Meanwhile, Papa X-Ray was back in business. A daily routine evolved. I'd pull up to the Lindsay Airpark, hop into the plane and take off for Buttonville. UPX seemed to know the route by heart. I'd listen to ATIS on 127.1 while I cut the northern edge off Sunderland, the southern edge off Uxbridge and hit Stouffville (pronounced stow – ville) just north of the water tower where I dialed up 124.8.

"Buttonville tower, Uniform Papa X-Ray."

"Papa X-Ray, Buttonville, go ahead."

"Buttonville tower, Uniform Papa X-Ray at two thousand over Stouffville VFR out of Lindsay for Buttonville with information bravo, over."

"Papa X-Ray, report by the three silos, not below two thousand."

Markham airport appeared off my left wing as I scanned ahead for the three silos. They were really hard to find the first time and then impossible to miss after that. As I came up to them, I noted the huge Greek Orthodox church to the northwest. Those gold spires were the next reporting point for a left hand base for one-five. Today, according to the ATIS, I'd get cleared to a right downwind three-three.

"Buttonville tower, Papa X-Ray at three silos."

"Papa X-Ray, cleared right hand downwind for three-three, report base." And so it would go until I floated past Michael's shop just east of the numbers at three-three, touched down long and turned off for the ramp. Ground control would clear me to the tie-downs where the folks at the Millionaire service centre would tie the airplane down and fuel it up when I needed it. Inside, I'd wave at the fuel desk and head out the door, briefcase in hand. The ten minute walk along the eastern edge of the field took me directly under the path of planes landing on two-one. Sometimes I'd sit on the rock ledge, lie back and watch their oily bellies fly overhead for a few minutes. Then I'd continue on, past Leggats, where I'd often pick up airplane supplies such as tires, oil or whatever might be needed back at Lindsay. Just beyond Leggats lay Michael's offices. I'd walk in and the receptionist would ask, "Did you fly in today, Jim?"

I'd answer, "I fly in every day."

Over the next year I took several of Michael's staff up for rides at one time or another. I'd make the tough guys sick by pulling negative and positive g's over Newmarket and treat the more timid souls to a lunchtime flight to Toronto Island and back. It was glorious. The Toronto city airspace was the most crowded in Canada and yet the easiest to navigate. Toronto Island tower was more than happy to let me ferry sightseers over the skyscrapers of Bay and King Streets or take a run at the skyline from the lake, shooting video footage for Michael's producers. More than once Papa X-Ray would have a miniature camera attached to its wing strut as we cruised up and down the Don Valley Parkway, capturing footage for videos.

The flight home was always as pleasant and relaxing as the flight in. I'd plunk down at Lindsay, pull up to the pumps, fuel up, park and head home. Just another day at the office. I logged more than 150 flights to Buttonville in UPX over the course of our first year in Cameron.

On weekends, Mary and Johnny would pile in for a flight to Brampton to visit Olive or head up to the cottage where we'd land at the Beaver Valley Soaring Club airstrip. Papa X-Ray was getting worked as a good 172 workhorse should. But its pilot was getting bored.

"What's a Cessna Hawk XP and why should I care?" Michael asked one day.

"It's sort of between a 172 and a 182 and it's a lot faster and a lot more powerful. You can care or not but I'm going to get me one of those," I answered, tapping a letter out in response to the classified ad: 1977 Hawk XPII, 850 TTSN.

The Entrepreneurship video series was completed and judged an unqualified success. Educational networks began broadcasting it across the country and teachers were welcoming a brand new resource for their new curriculum. The teacher in me was pleased. And once again it was a time of beginnings and endings. I began to do speaking engagements for CFEE, criss-crossing the country to introduce our new series to teachers from coast to coast. I was ready for new challenges and a new plane.

"But why do we need a different plane?" Mary wanted to know. "This one is paid for and it works well. And you just did the engine two years ago."

"I'm getting bored is why," I answered. Knowing I'd need to come up with a better reason, I continued. "Boredom leads to complacency. And complacency can be dangerous for a 500-hour pilot…"

"And this XP thing would be better?"

"Sure, it will be safer and faster." Johnny's eyes lit up, "And it will be a lot newer and cleaner and red, white and blue instead of, you know…"

"But it will cost more money, right?"

"But now that we have our company going again, we can write off the expenses of owning it so we'll save money on taxes." Saving money by buying a new plane. I had to admit that was a clincher if ever there was one.

"So you'll be selling Papa X-Ray, then?"

"Well, we don't need two planes, do we?"

"Ahhh. It will be sad to see her go," Mary said, sounding as though we were about to auction off our only son who was now an old flying pro and already getting bored with any and all kinds of airplanes. Except maybe faster ones.

It would be sad to see her go. It panged my heart, no question. But I wanted more horsepower. I wanted a constant-speed prop and I wanted never again to experience white-knuckles when lifting off over fences at gross weight in the summer. A Cessna 182 was too much plane, too heavy, too hungry for fuel. The Hawk XP would be perfect. I placed an ad for Papa X-Ray and within a week, two fellows from Oshawa showed up, went for a ride and wrote a cheque.

Just like that. I choked up as they flew my baby away to the south. The cheque in my pocket felt like thirty pieces of silver. But the feeling didn't last long. Papa X-Ray had a new owner and a new home and would be living relatively close by. Dry those eyes.

Two months and many thousands of dollars later…

"Well? What do you think?"

"I love the colour!"

"Yeah, it's nice, Dad," John, who was no longer Johnny, said as he stepped on the bright red wheel pant and into the blue interior of our new Hawk XP. "This is really nice, Dad. It smells better than our old plane."

"Let's go for a ride!" Mary popped into the front seat and closed the door. "Ooohhh. I love these fancy door latches," she cooed as she pushed the long chrome levers into place in the armrest. "Nice radios, too…it's so new!"

I lined up for three-one. "Lindsay traffic, Papa Charlie Uniform departing, straight out."

"Papa Charlie Uniform? That sounds so strange after hearing Uniform Papa X-Ray for so many years," Mary commented.

I turned to her and smiled. "Get ready for a whole new flying experience." I threw on full power, all one hundred and ninety-five horses of it. With the prop at full fine pitch and 2600 rpm on the tachometer, the plane pitched forward like it was shot out of a catapult. The engine howled.

"Whooooeeeee!" Mary shouted through the intercom.

I hauled back on the yoke and the nose pitched up until the breaker panel lined up with the horizon. The Vertical Speed Indicator pegged at fifteen hundred feet per minute initial climb rate.

"Dad! My ears!" John called from the back seat. I leveled off and took up a heading of west southwest.

"Well?" I asked, proudly.

"I love it, Jim," Mary answered, as she unfolded the chart on her lap. "Where are we going?"

"How about heading to Brampton to show Olive?" I said, noting a solid 120 knots indicated with the prop and throttle set at 23 squared. What a honey of a machine! I dialed up 126.7 on one of the two RT 328Ts to file a plan. Two radios!

"That would mean we should be heading a little more north." Mary scanned the horizon and then checked her chart. Some things never changed. I adjusted the heading just in time to hear a familiar transmission.

"Mary, listen to this! Listen John!" A voice crackled through the big speaker overhead.

"Roger, Toronto radio, this is Uniform Papa X-Ray, over."

"Hey, it's old Papa X-Ray!" Mary shouted. I couldn't help myself. I keyed the push-to-talk on my new yoke.

"Toronto radio this is Papa Charlie Uniform. Would you mind if I cut in and said 'hello' to our old plane for a minute?"

"Go ahead Charlie Uniform."

"Papa X-Ray, it's Papa Charlie Uniform. How's the good old bird treating you?"

"Charlie Uniform. Hi Jim. We just love her. She's a great airplane. Thanks for letting her go."

"Our pleasure, Papa X-Ray. I hope you chalk up as many good memories with her as we did. Charlie Uniform out." I glanced at Mary who just smiled and turned back to John, who seemed a little mystified, but only a little.

"When are we going to get to Grandma's, Dad?" he asked, opening his lunch box and fishing out a cookie.

# Enjoy other books from Happy Landings

### *Fly Yellow Side Up* by Garth Wallace
A humorous story of a suburban flying instructor who moves up north to seek the freedom and glory of bush flying. It is the ideal situation for a city slicker to make a fool of himself. You won't be disappointed.

### *Pie In The Sky* by Garth Wallace
Ride with Wallace as he discovers cowboy ag-pilots, Mennonite buggy buzzing and other off-the-wall aviation adventures. The second in a series of three funny flying books by Wallace.

### *Derry Air* by Garth Wallace
In "Derry Air", flying instructor Wallace meets the wonderfully sarcastic ground school instructor, "Dutch", linecrew Huey, Duey and Louey, a horse that flies and the most odd-ball collection of student pilots ever assembled at one flying school.

### *Blue Collar Pilots* by Garth Wallace
A lighthearted tribute to the low-profile cockpit grunts who don't fly airplanes that fly themselves. It is a collection of one-liners, jokes and anecdotes that celebrates blue collar aviation.

### *Don't Call Me a Legend* by Garth Wallace
Charlie Vaughn is Canada's most famous modern day aviator. The book is a legacy of aviation stories about how Vaughn worked his way from flying farm boy to world renowned ferry pilot.

## Available at book stores or directly from:
Happy Landings            Tel.: 613-269-2552
RR # 4                 Fax: 613-269-3962
Merrickville, Ontario   Web site: www.happylanding.com
Canada, K0G 1N0      E-mail: books@happylanding.com

# About the author

From 1975 to 1985, Saskatchewan-born Jim Lang (guitar) and Ontario's own Mary Ackroyd (fiddle) lived their dream in the music business. After ten years on the road from Los Angeles to Whitehorse to Frankfurt, Jim and Mary were joined by little Johnny, who, although only an infant, encouraged them to hang up their instruments and slow down a little. So, Jim dusted off his old teaching certificate and headed the family north.

After three years of teaching and flying in the Northwest Territories from 1985 to1988, Jim and Mary moved to Cameron, Ontario, a twenty-five minute flight northeast of Toronto (by Cessna 172.) The Lang & Ackroyd Band became Lang & Ackroyd Productions, Inc., which focused on producing entrepreneurship education and training resources. Ten years later, their company has four television series, two CD-ROMs and dozens of smaller productions to its credit. And somewhere along the way, Jim became a writer of books.

Papa X-Ray represents a light-hearted change for Jim as an author. His two other books in current international release, Make Your Own Breaks and Great Careers for People Who Want to be Entrepreneurs, deal with the more serious issue of taking control of one's life and work in an uncertain world. In addition to writing and producing, today Jim is in growing demand as an entertaining motivational speaker. Cyberspace visitors to Lang & Ackroyd Productions are welcome at http://www.jlang.com.

Jim is still flying. Two airplanes followed Papa X-Ray, C-GPCU, a 1977 Cessna Hawk XPII and Jim's current plane, C-FRZZ, a cherry 1960 Cessna 210 which he keeps at the Lindsay Airpark, in Lindsay, Ontario. Jim and Mary's son, John – no longer "Johnny" – is now a teen-aged basketball fanatic. Having outgrown his mother, he now sits in the copilot seat, while Mary navigates from the back. After logging more than 1000 hours in the air since the age of three, John still can't figure out "what all the fuss is about."